Homeowner's Guide to Landscaping

Raymond Felice

Ideals Publishing Corp.
Milwaukee, Wisconsin

Table of Contents

ISBN 0-8249-6117-X

Copyright © 1982 by Ideals Publishing Corporation

All rights reserved. This book or parts thereof, may not be reproduced in any form without permission of the copyright owner. Printed and bound in the United States of America. Published simultaneously in Canada.

Published by Ideals Publishing Corporation
11315 Watertown Plank Road
Milwaukee, Wisconsin 53226

Editor, David Schansberg

Cover photo courtesy of Hedrich-Blessing.

ACKNOWLEDGMENTS
Thomson's Nursery and Garden Center, Rt. 1, Danvers, Massachusetts 01923. True Temper, 1623 Euclid Avenue, Cleveland, Ohio 44115. California Redwood Association, 617 Montgomery Street, San Francisco, California 94111. Walpole Woodworkers, Rt. 129, Wilmington, Massachusetts 01887. Swivelier Company Inc., Nanuet, New York 10954. Appleton Electric Company, 1701 Wellington Avenue, Chicago, Illinois 60657. de Jager Bulbus, Inc., 188 Asbury St., S. Hamilton, Massachusetts 01982. Russell Associates, Lynn, Massachusetts. Wayne Stonkus, Peabody, Massachusetts. Louis Mangifesti, Reading, Massachusetts. J. Farmer Landscape Co., Inc., Middleton, Massachusetts. A special thank you to Robert Thomson and Ronald Swanson of Thomson's Nursery and Garden Center for all their help with designs and with the coordination of all material.

Introduction

How can you maximize your family's enjoyment of the yard? How can you make your lawn greener and more attractive? How can you make the weekly chores of mowing and trimming easier? How can you plant and maintain a vegetable garden that will produce a good harvest? These are but a few of the questions that this book will answer.

Landscaping Objectives

People are often discouraged by landscaping projects because they expect to see results overnight. It takes several years for landscaping to achieve the ultimate results. By following a realistic plan, however, you can (1) in time create a landscape that not only looks beautiful but adds to the family's enjoyment of your outdoor living space, (2) establish lawns and gardens that are easily maintained, and (3) increase the value of your property.

With the detailed guidelines presented here, you can design a landscape that provides areas for sun, shade, barbecues, vegetable and flower gardens, and areas for play and relaxation. This book offers suggestions for: seeding your lawn; planting trees, shrubs, and gardens; building patios; and attracting birds. The objective will be to adapt your home's landscape to successfully meet your family's needs and interests.

Once established, your yard will need only basic weekly maintenance to ensure that the grounds remain appealing to the eye. The key to successful maintenance is simple—eliminate trouble before it begins by planning wisely and selecting the correct tools, plants, fertilizers, and pesticides.

Landscaping expenditures of up to 2 percent of the total cost of your house and property can easily be recovered when you sell your property. For example, if you purchased your home for $70,000, you can spend up to $1,400 on landscaping, knowing you will probably be reimbursed when you sell your house. In fact, you will probably increase the resale price by up to $5,000, because a knowledgeable buyer will appreciate the value of the time, effort, and materials represented in your landscaping effort. Landscaping enhances the home and property and can help persuade a potential home buyer to purchase your home.

Basic Steps for Successful Landscaping

Advance planning is essential. Make a list of all the things that you expect from your yard, decide how much area is needed for each of your activities, put your plan on paper, and then go outside and stake out each area to make sure that it will accommodate your expectations. Are there good landscape designers available in your area to assist you? Visit your local agricultural school and seek information about various designs and materials. If you plan to design the yard yourself, read as many trade magazines and data sheets as possible to maximize your available space.

Visit your local nursery to find out what species will grow in your region, your neighborhood, and in your particular soil. Find out how local weather conditions will affect certain plants and insects which may plague your area. It may be necessary to forego some varieties of grass, plants, and trees rather than waste your valuable time and money on a futile project.

Carefully estimate how much time and money you can afford to spend on your project and follow those figures each year. Consider, too, how soon you expect to have the project completed. Don't plant a shrub that takes twenty years to mature if you want it fully grown in five. If you plan to stay in your home indefinitely, you have all the time you need to develop your outdoor living areas, but if you expect to move within two or three years, plan accordingly; otherwise, you may never see the fulfillment of your plans.

Landscape Design

Planning your outdoor living space is just as important to full enjoyment of your home as interior design and should take into consideration the aesthetic as well as functional needs of each family member. Whether relandscaping or developing a new homesite, the planning phase can be an exciting family experience and, if properly done, can increase the value of your property as well as save future time and money on yard maintenance.

Drafting Your Plan

The final graphic representation of a yard can be as sophisticated as a professional landscape architect's rendering or as informal as a pencil sketch. At the outset, however, you will need to draw the plot plan to scale; that is, preserve in your illustration the shape of the plot but reduce each line according to a fixed ratio. On the drawing, you should note the scale being used. Square-ruled or graph paper will simplify this task. Measure the house and locate it accurately on the plan, noting doors and windows and their height from the ground because their location will govern the sizes and types of plants you will use around the foundation. Also include all other fixed structures, such as the driveway, walks, and plantings.

With this basic diagram before you—and perhaps a few copies of it for sketching various designs—it is time to consider your family's life-style and what your final design should include to suit your needs and your particular site. Indicate areas for each of these general purposes: utility space, living area, gardens, and play area. Then plan each area in light of the size of your lot, the limitations of your budget, and your family's interests and priorities.

Utility Areas Is there adequate space in your garage and basement for storing yard tools, lawn furniture, and the charcoal grill? If not, your plan should allow space for the construction of a garden shed. Plan convenient locations for clothesline and trash barrels, so they can be attractively concealed or at least not be in the way of living and play space.

Living Areas Here you can give free rein to your imagination if your lot size and pocketbook allow. At a minimum, plan for a patio or lawn area for outdoor relaxation. If a swimming pool is contemplated, even well in the future, plan for it now rather than having to cut down beloved trees and shrubs later. If you have pets, don't overlook them in your

scheme. Plan for fences, dog houses, and other pet shelters, keeping in mind the safety of pets and the preservation of your lawn, plants, and shrubs.

Garden Areas Plan space for rock gardens, flower beds, and vegetable gardens, which are discussed in detail later in this book.

Play Areas Children should have a safe open play area and will enjoy a sandbox and swing set. For teenagers and adults, consider an area for badminton, croquet, horseshoes, volleyball, or other favorite games.

If you are relandscaping, it is wise to make a checklist of what already exists and what is needed before drawing your final plan so you will not omit any desired changes. The checklist will also help your nurseryman or professional landscaper choose what is right for you.

Completing Your Design

An abundance of material is available to assist you with your overall design, whether you plan to do the work yourself or hire a professional landscape architect. Newspapers, especially the Sunday editions, usually have a garden section which gives not only regional planting and fertilizing information but also occasional designs that can be easily adapted to your own plans. Trade magazines like *Flower and Garden* and other regional publications provide a wealth of information on planning, maintenance, new products, and the treatment of problems. Seed and flower catalogs also provide useful design information. U.S. Government publications are available at no or low cost and cover the whole spectrum of home landscaping.

Perhaps the most valuable source of assistance is your local nurseryman, who is usually willing to discuss your design and advise you on plant selection. He also carries quantities of trade pamphlets, which are usually free.

In choosing your plantings, there are five basic considerations: soil, climate, existing structures,

The first design illustration (opposite, above left) is a drawing of the plot plan to scale indicating house, drive, walk, existing patio and property lines. Make several copies of this drawing. On one of the copies indicate existing plants and trees, slopes, views, wind directions, sun directions, and other existing features (opposite, above right). On another scale drawing plan your new landscape, indicating all plants and new structures (opposite below).

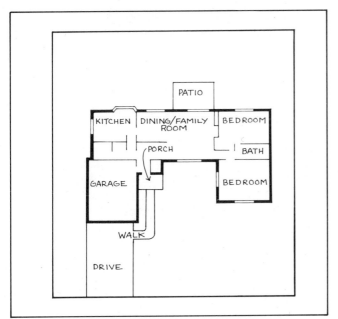

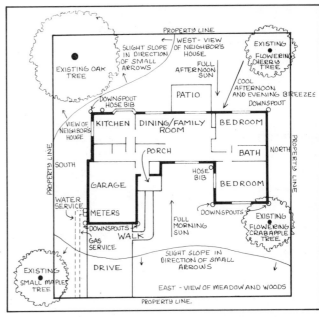

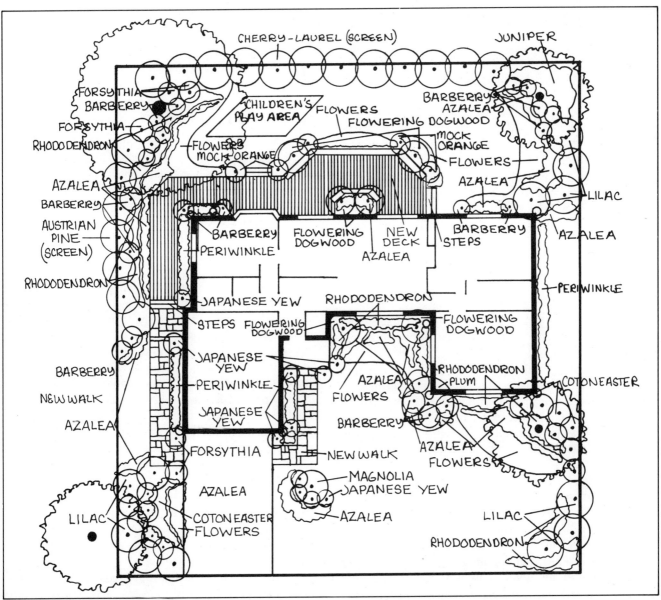

topography, and the aesthetic effect you want.

Soil It is important to know what type of soil you have—sand, clay, adobe, or loam—and to choose plants that will adapt well. Soil that is made up of about 60 percent clay deprives plant roots of oxygen and will not absorb water. Soil that is approximately 70 percent sand allows water to pass through it quickly, stripping the soil of nutrients, and dries out quickly. Adobe is a heavy clay soil found in the hot, dry regions of the country. It cannot retain water and cracks when it dries out. Loam, which is made up of 40 percent sand, 40 percent silt, and 20 percent clay, is considered the perfect soil for growing plants.

A complete soil analysis at your local agricultural school or nursery will determine your soil type, whether the soil is lacking any nutriments, and how it can be improved. Soil should be retested every four years to make sure that it stays consistent. Home soil-testing kits are excellent for quick checks, but do not give the complete analysis you will need at the outset. If your soil presents a real problem, it may be necessary to add soil or even replace it completely.

Climate Know the temperature range in your area. It is essential that you choose only plants that can withstand the climate, or you will be faced with costly replacements. Also check the average rainfall in your area and, if needed, make arrangements to supply water.

Structures The size and shape of your house should be considered so plantings will be in proportion to the house, will complement its architectural lines, and will provide a visually pleasing transition between the house and its site. Determine how your house is located in relation to the sun, wind, and structures such as a shed or swimming pool. Then you can decide whether you need shaded areas around the house or more exposure. Properly placed trees can cut down on penetrating winds during the winter and cool the house during hot summer months.

Topography Take advantage of any natural features of the land like small streams, inclines, or large rocks. These can become the focal point of your yard. A small stream can become a formal sitting area when planted with shrubs and clusters of flowers along the bank. An incline can be terraced and planted with low-growing flowers, shrubs, and ground cover. Large rock formations can become an impressive rock garden. If existing conditions do not allow these features to fit into your overall plan, it is possible, but expensive, to have the topography of your lot rearranged.

However, steps must be taken to preserve existing trees that will be either above or below the new grade. A tree well can be constructed of concrete blocks to allow the root system of a below-grade tree to receive water and nutrients. The soil that supports the root system of an above-grade tree can be retained by a wall constructed of treated wood, brick, or precast concrete blocks.

Aesthetic Effect For all practical purposes, there are only three basic landscaping designs: formal, informal, and a blending of both.

Formal landscaping has its origin in the colonial period. This design employs well-defined planting areas with straight, neatly trimmed rows. Formal design is still very popular in many historic southern areas, where there is little variety in the climate. To attain the desired symmetry, you will have to divide your area in half with an imaginary line and exactly duplicate on one side whatever is planted on the other side.

The informal design is also balanced, but not necessarily symmetrical. It is achieved by grouping plants on each side by size and color. This design is by far the most popular design used today because of its natural, free-flowing look.

A combination of formal and informal design is difficult to achieve and should not be attempted by a beginner without seeking professional advice.

Landscaping Guidelines

Make sure your finished product will give balance to the lot, not overpower it. For example, if yours is a single-story house, choose trees that grow to a height of 20 to 30 feet, such as members of the crab and dogwood family. For taller houses, taller trees are acceptable.

Do not overcrowd the plants. It is better to have too few plants than too many, so that they have space to grow and thrive.

Select a good mixture of plants, and avoid uniformity of size and color to give appealing contrast to the yard. Although evergreens are most often used as foundation plantings, consider incorporating some deciduous plants in the overall scheme to add color and beauty. The wildlife, who will feed on flowers and berries, will also benefit.

Keep plantings around doorways small and simple. Evergreens are an excellent choice because they require only occasional pruning. In heavy traffic areas, construct walkways of bricks, flagstones, cement, railroad ties, or wooden rounds to eliminate reseeding each year.

On slight inclines create a rock garden of phlox, vines, or ivy. This will add beauty to your yard and eliminate the risk of mowing an area that is not level. Steep slopes are best terraced utilizing rock gardens and small plantings.

Dress driveways with a low border of annual (live one year) or perennial flowers (live from year to

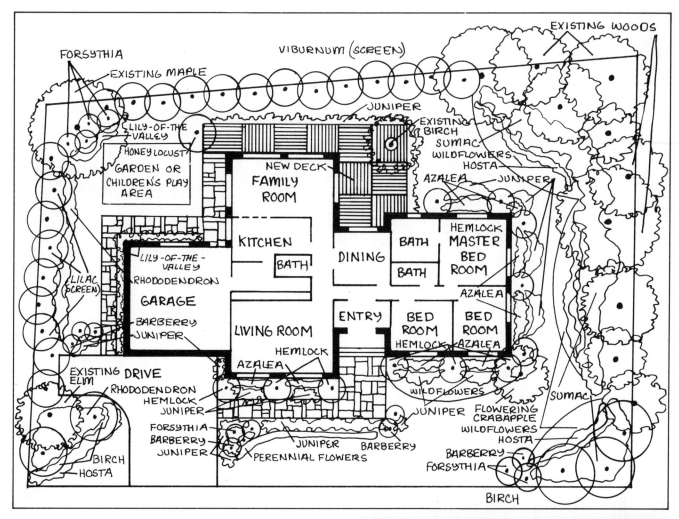

The above drawing is another example of a finished landscape design showing all plants, trees, and shrubs in their final planned positions.

year) on each side. A few small evergreens or shrubs placed at the entrance will add dimension to the planting.

Edge out a circle around each shade tree and fill it with peat moss, mulch, or small stones to protect the surface roots from the lawn mower blade. Planting a ground cover or a variety of flowers in the circle will add a color accent to the yard.

Set off flower beds with either a mowing strip or edge and fill with mulch, peat moss, or stone to cut down on the weeding. It will also help protect flowers from being bruised or damaged by the lawn mower.

Include in your design a balanced mixture of shrubs (evergreen and flowering), trees (proper height), and flowers that will bloom at different times during the season to give continuous color and variety to your landscape.

Carrying Out Your Plan

Will You Do the Work Yourself? Before you decide whether you will complete the landscaping

Shrubs delicately balanced with clusters of flowers will greatly enhance your pool area.

yourself or hire a professional for part or all of it, consider the size and topography of the lot and the time, tools, and money required for the project. If the yard is relatively small (5 to 10 thousand square feet) and you plan only minor cosmetic work, it is feasible to complete the job yourself. If your lot is 15

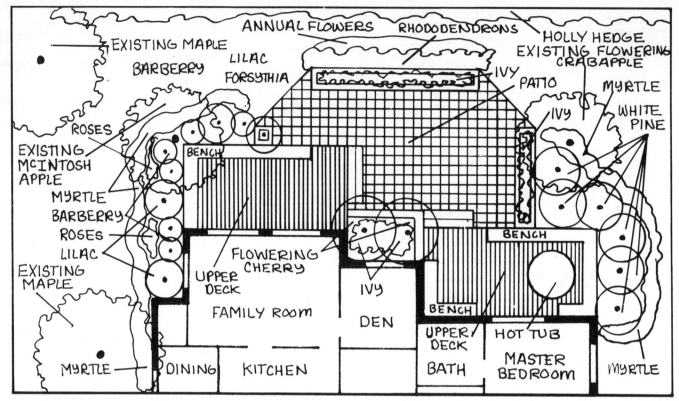

This drawing is the final design for an elaborate outdoor living area. Two raised wood decks, one off the family room and one off the master bedroom (with a hot tub), lead to a lower patio area level with the surrounding land. Brick planters enclose the patio area somewhat. Taller white pines are used to provide privacy for hot tub users.

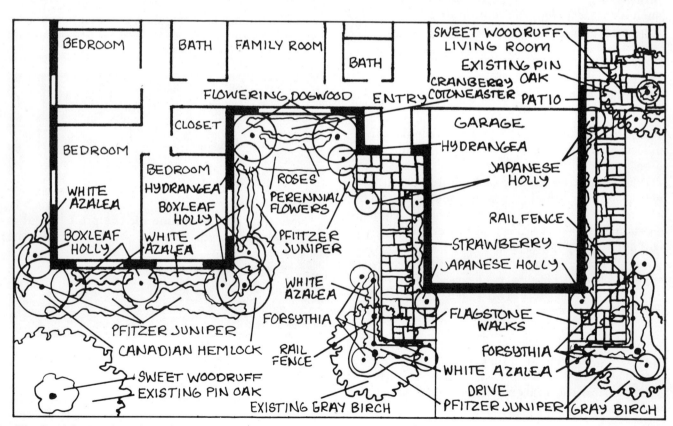

The final design for a front foundation planting features an excellent mix of evergreens, flowering shrubs, and flowers. Perennial everbearing strawberries were planted as ground cover along both walks to provide beauty and delicious, sweet fruit.

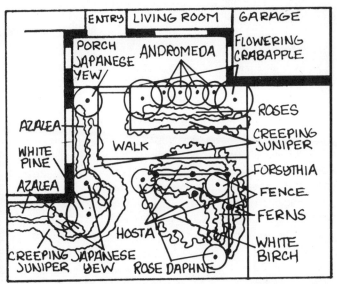

The drawings on this page show how two different types of approach areas were landscaped. The home in the drawing at left has the front entrance a few feet above the drive level. Two sets of steps and a brick walk, patio, and series of retaining walls are used to draw visitors to the front entrance. The approach area in the drawing at right is level with the main entrance to this ranch-style home. A group of shrubs and trees around a post-and-rail fence screens the home from car lights.

to 60 thousand square feet or if the topography must be altered, for example, by moving low hills or regrading the entire surface, it is advisable to seriously consider using a professional for at least part of the work.

Do you have the time to devote to the job to ensure professional results? Even a small planting job, such as a 4 x 20-foot foundation area, can be very time-consuming. You may have to browse through several garden centers to purchase the proper plants for your design. Preparing the area (raking, weeding, fertilizing, edging), planting, and adding decorative chips or stones could take up to sixteen hours. Regrading a small 40 x 60-foot yard could require twelve hours to turn the soil, rough-grade, level, seed, roll, and water. If you are not sure how long your particular project will take, consult your local nurseryman or landscaper.

For the average small planting area you will require a pitchfork, pointed shovel, metal rake, edger, hoe, trowel, and wheelbarrow. If you are planning a major change in your landscaping that involves moving slight inclines, cutting down trees, trucking in large amounts of loam, or moving rocks, you will need to rent a roller, grader, and chain saw. For this type of project, you must acknowledge your limitations and consider hiring a professional.

Small shrubs can cost anywhere from $5 to $50, and larger ones can range upward from $80. If you want to figure how much it would cost for your particular project, ask several landscapers for written estimates on materials and labor (most reputable landscapers charge between $15 and $20 per hour for labor). Compare their estimates with what it would cost you to purchase the plants yourself plus about $7 per hour for your own labor. Decide if

the amount you will save by doing it yourself is worthwhile.

Let's compare the cost of a 4 x 30-foot foundation planting using an arbitrary figure of $10 per shrub:

YOU	
15 plants at $10 each	$150
Labor, 18 hours at $7 per hour	$126
TOTAL	$276
LANDSCAPER	
15 plants at $10 each	$150
Labor, 10 hours at $15 per hour	$150
TOTAL	$300

Note that the labor time for the professional is less than your own. This should hold true for the better, well-equipped firms. Note also that there is a saving of only $24. So unless you are willing to donate your time and effort to the job, the total savings may not be worthwhile.

Selecting a Professional If you plan to contract the work to a professional, choose carefully. Usually word of mouth is the professional's best advertisement, but if you do not know of one by reputation, ask several concerns for written estimates and compare the prices. If possible, ask to see some of their recent work so you may judge its quality. Select only a landscaper who will guarantee all plants and labor for a reasonable amount of time after the work is completed.

Lawns

Selecting the Seed

A good seed is one that contains very little weed or what manufacturers call "crop." The Department of Agriculture publishes a list of all grass seeds sold in the United States. However, it is wise to learn from your local nursery which grass will grow best in your area. The following is a partial list of the more popular lawn grasses:

Bluegrass This excellent grass is the most widely used for home lawns in northern areas. It grows slower than most but will withstand many common diseases. There are about twenty types of bluegrass, and all need at least partial sun to thrive.

Fescue This member of the bluegrass family will adapt to poor soil conditions, shade, and areas of little water (upper South, Midwest, and North). The three most popular types of fescue are Jamestown, a type that has underground stems that multiply and that does not have rhizomes; Ruby, a creeping fescue that does produce rhizomes; and tall fescue, which will stay green longer than the previous two but is restricted to shaded areas.

Ryegrass Good for use in northern states, these grasses grow quicker than the others, and many of the newer types are quite attractive. The annual ryegrass, sold as domestic or Italian ryegrass, is excellent for starting a new lawn. However, most of the lawn will not survive the winter if it is not reseeded in the fall with a better seed. Many contractors use annual ryegrass when building new homes because it is inexpensive and will grow rapidly. If you are planning to purchase a new home, it would be wise to learn what type of grass has been used. The perennial ryegrasses are most desirable because they will continue to grow year after year. Perhaps the most attractive and hardy of these are the newest types, Pennifine and Manhattan, which have fine blades and look like the better bluegrass.

Bermuda The improved varieties of Bermuda grasses thrive in the full sunlight of southern states. Because of their smooth, even-textured blades, they are used extensively on many golf courses. However, they are plagued by many lawn insects, such as sod webworms and nematodes.

St. Augustine This most popular grass of the Gulf area (Florida to Texas) does well in both sun and shade. It will do well even along the salt water shores where most other grasses fail.

Zoysia This new type of grass is still most popular in the midsouthern states, but it is starting to catch on elsewhere. It is a fine-textured, slow-growing grass that is planted as "plugs." Although this grass is bothered by sod webworms and nematodes, it needs very little care once it is established. With occasional fertilizing, it will even withstand drought conditions.

Your Own Seed Mixture Sometimes you will find that mixing your own seeds will produce a much healthier lawn, especially in the cold regions where there is a drastic change in climate. An excellent mixture would be one-third annual ryegrass to quickly establish a temporary lawn; one-third bluegrass for a virtually disease-free permanent lawn; and one-third fescue, which will adapt to most soil conditions and become part of the permanent lawn. However, in warmer regions where there is little climate variation, mixing grass seeds is unnecessary.

Starting a New Lawn

The prime requisites for establishing a beautiful new lawn are proper soil preparation, good quality seed, and proper, consistent care. Tools that you will need include a shovel, wheelbarrow, a drop-action spreader, a steel rake, a lawn and leaf rake, and a light roller. Your lawn can be successfully planted if you follow these basic steps:

1. Remove all debris, roots, stones, and the like from the area. Prepare the soil by loosening it to a depth of 2 to 4 inches either by rototilling or using a steel rake. If this is done properly, the surface will provide crevices where the new grass seedlings can be protected from the elements and gain a foothold.

2. Grade the area with the steel rake making sure it is as flat as possible. If you are grading around a house, be sure to pitch the grade slightly away from the house to allow water to flow away from the foundation.

3. Fertilize with a "starter fertilizer" that has a ratio of 18-24-6 (nitrogen-phosphorus-potash). If this is not available, the type used for vegetable gardens will produce the same results. Next, apply lime (about 50 pounds per 1000 square feet) to sweeten the soil.

4. Seed the area following the coverage instructions on the spreader or seed package. If no information is available, use two or three pounds of seed per 1000 square feet. Sow the seed evenly over the entire area, then go over it

Steps in starting a new lawn: 1. Prepare soil by loosening to a depth of 4 inches, removing all stones and debris; 2. Grade the area with a steel rake; 3. Fertilize and apply lime; 4. After seeding, roll the lawn with a light roller.

again at right angles to your original flow to ensure complete coverage.

5. Using a lawn and leaf rake, cover the seed lightly to a depth not over ¼ inch. A deeper cover may retard germination. Then go over the area with a light roller (not filled with water) to bring the seed into contact with the soil. If a roller is not available, the seed should be "walked" into the soil, although this method will not give as consistent soil contact.

6. Water with a fine mist three times a day if possible—in the morning, early afternoon, and evening. If the midday watering cannot be done, the lawn certainly should be watered twice a day to prevent it from drying out.

7. Cut your lawn when it reaches a height of 1½ to 2 inches. It is important to use a grass bag or to rake the lawn lightly, to avoid suffocating the new seedlings.

8. After the first cutting, water every other day except during dry weather. Then water as needed.

9. About four weeks after the first cutting, fertilize again with a regular fertilizer (10-6-4) to keep your new lawn green and ensure proper root development.

Reseeding a Poor Lawn

Often, a thin or poor lawn can be thickened by seeding over the existing grass, which involves approximately half the time and money of turning over the old lawn and achieves twice the number of grass plants. Reseeding can be done any time of the year, but it is generally recommended in the early spring or early fall when soil and weather conditions are perfect for establishing new seedlings.

First, mow your lawn as short as possible without scalping it. Then, using a lawn and leaf rake, scratch the soil to remove any debris that has accumulated and to make small crevices, no deeper than ¼ inch, where the seed can lodge itself to germinate. In extreme cases, when the soil is too com-

pacted, a power rake may be necessary. This tool is available through most rental services.

To disperse the seed over larger lawn areas, use a drop-action spreader (a rotary-type spreader will not distribute the grass seed evenly). On smaller areas the seed may be spread more efficiently by hand. If you wish to fertilize the new grass seedlings to help the germination process, consult your local dealer for the proper mixture. The wrong mixture can kill or damage the seed. "Starter fertilizers" are your best bet.

Perhaps the most important part of reseeding your lawn is keeping the new seedlings moist until they are well established. By following steps 6, 7, and 8 for starting a new lawn you should produce a thick and rich-looking lawn. If any problems do arise, consult your local garden nursery or landscaper.

Bare Spots

The most common reasons for bare spots are poor drainage, improper seed mixtures, compacted soil, and insect damage. Your specific problem can be determined as follows:

Poor Drainage Water collects or soil washes away in heavy rain.

Improper Seed Mixture Cheaper seed that keeps dying out or seed that requires sun but is planted in a shady area.

Compacted Soil Water runs off without penetrating the soil, and lawn and leaf rakes will not scratch the soil surface.

Insect Damage Most apt to occur in hot, dry weather; small lawn moths are seen flying low above the grass in the early evening; brown areas can be rolled up in carpet-fashion; or the lawn starts to die in a spreading manner.

If you suspect insect damage, it would be wise to take a sample to your local nursery or agricultural school for analysis to determine the proper treatment needed to restore your lawn to a healthy state.

After you have determined why your lawn has

failed, loosen the soil about ½ inch with a steel rake, spade (square shovel), or cultivating tool. Spread the seed and fertilizer by hand and then cover lightly using a lawn and leaf rake. Keep the spots moist until the new seed germinates.

Regrading

Regrading is sometimes necessary. Most often this is the result of overlooking or misinterpreting drainage problems which may not be evident until after the first heavy rain. Minor regrading can generally be accomplished by simply topdressing the area with additional soil. However, by following the steps below any regrading problem can be solved.

1. Determine the amount of additional soil required. It may be necessary to level high areas. This soil can be used to fill in other areas.
2. Determine where drainage should be directed, keeping in mind that your grade must slope away from the foundation of the house.
3. After adding the additional soil, simply reseed as explained in the previous section.

Sodding

Although sodding is initially more expensive than seeding, its advantages make it extremely worthwhile. Not only does it instantly increase property value, but it produces a lawn that is weed-free and requires less attention than newly seeded lawns. Sodding also solves the problem of seeding high-traffic areas. It is best to rely on a professional landscaper who guarantees his product, but a do-it-yourselfer can do it with a minimum of effort following these steps:

1. Measure the square footage of the area accurately. The best way to minimize waste (sod is very expensive) is to divide the area into squares or rectangles. A strip of sod is 1½ x 6 feet (nine square feet).
2. Prepare the area by following the first three steps described earlier in this chapter for starting a new lawn.
3. Begin by laying the sod along a straight edge, such as a driveway or walk. Stagger the strips so the seams are not in a straight line.
4. With a sharp knife or edging tool cut pieces to fit around trees, flower beds, and posts.
5. Use a roller on the sod area to ensure proper soil contact.
6. Soak the lawn for one to one and one-half hours. Thereafter, water about once every other day.

After two or three weeks your lawn should be well established. Until then, your new lawn will accept only light traffic. Mowing can first be done six or seven days after the sod has been laid or when the grass reaches a height of 2 to 2½ inches. New sod should not be cut below a height of 1½ inches. Fertilizing should be done three times a year, but you should consult your dealer for the proper times and fertilizer to use. Lime may be spread once a year at a rate of 25 pounds per 1000 square feet, half of that normally used for a newly seeded lawn.

Lawn Maintenance

Proper lawn maintenance serves a twofold purpose. First it will save you time. Once the lawn area has been set up for the season you can figure exactly how much time it will take you each week to maintain its beauty and you can eliminate some of the problems, like crabgrass and insects, before they gain a foothold. Second, it will save you money in the long run. For example, it is better to spend a few dollars at the beginning of the season to prevent various lawn insects than to spend hundreds of dollars later to have the entire lawn dug up, treated, and reseeded.

Take pride in your lawn and be good to it. The beautiful results will be worth the effort.

Cutting Fescue, bluegrass, and St. Augustine grass should be cut to a height of 1½ to 2½ inches to allow the formation of a deep root system that will not dry out in the hot sun. If the lawn is cut too short, the roots will not form the rhizomes that are needed to thicken and multiply the grass blades. All other grasses such as the Bermuda, bent grass, and zoysia should be cut to a height of 1 to 1½ inches. Unless you are willing to baby your lawn as the professionals do, cut it no shorter than the recommended height.

Mow regularly—at least once a week. If you delay too long, the lawn will turn a yellowish color from lack of chlorophyll and be vulnerable to crabgrass and weed invasion. If this should happen, it will take about two weeks for your lawn to recover.

Don't cut with a dull mower. If the tips of the grass blades are ragged and uneven, it is time to have your mower blade sharpened.

If you use a grass bag, start to mow at the outside edge of the longest length of lawn to eliminate the needless turns. Divide a lawn that is not fairly square into sections or squares, then proceed to cut.

If you do not use a grass bag, make your first cut down the center of the lawn and proceed to cut in widening circles so that the grass is always discharged toward the outside edges of the lawn. Any time spent in overlapping the ends of the rows will be saved when you will have to rake only the edges rather than the entire lawn.

Fertilizing Perhaps the most valuable aid to landscaping and gardening is the use of a compost pile. Organic materials such as grass clippings,

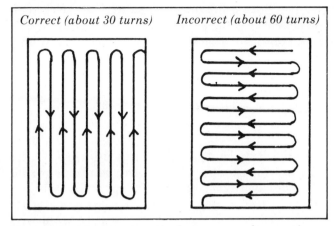

Correct (about 30 turns)   *Incorrect (about 60 turns)*

Correct and incorrect methods to mow a lawn using a lawn bag.

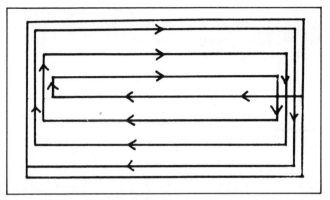

Mowing plan when not using a grass bag

leaves, and shrub prunings are piled into thin layers, which when oxidized will become rich slow-release fertilizer for plantings or simply for enriching the soil.

There are three basic composting methods. The first and easiest method is to discard materials in a compost pile. However, it will take about one to two years before it is ready for use, and if left unattended, the compost can produce an offensive odor.

A faster and more efficient method is to discard materials in a compost bin made of logs, snow fence, chicken wire, or rocks. Build the bin on a clear area of ground at least 3 feet square, leaving one side accessible for removal of the finished product. Then place a layer of stone or twigs inside the floor of the bin to allow air to flow from underneath the material. Add a 6- to 12-inch layer of clippings and cover with a 1- to 2-inch layer of soil. Dampen the pile and repeat the layers until enough heat is generated to stimulate the bacteria into oxidizing the material. As your pile becomes compressed by settling and decomposition, turn and loosen it with a pitchfork to allow more air to circulate. If the pile seems dry or gray in color, add more water after turning.

The neatest and most popular way of composting is the closed container method. Containers with intake and exhaust doors to allow quick and easy access to the composted material are sold in nurseries for about $40. If you are a do-it-yourselfer, a smaller container can be made by using a metal garbage can. To do this, clear an area the diameter of the can and place a layer of rocks in the clearing. Then perforate the bottom and sides of the container to allow for aeration. Set the container on the rocks, and you are ready to begin your compost pile.

If correctly stored and maintained, compost ripens quickly and odorlessly. The presence of meat, fat, and vegetable waste in the compost may attract insects and rodents, but if you omit such wastes, these pests will not bother you.

Granular-type fertilizer is preferable for fertilizing lawns because it can be applied evenly, with only a minimal chance of the wind blowing it off its mark. Liquid fertilizers, usually applied with a spray bottle, are excellent for trees, hedges, and bushes because they can reach the inside of the plant around the trunk area. They are especially helpful in controlling insects in places where they could multiply if left unchecked.

The common belief that the spring is the only time to fertilize is untrue. Most lawns are composed of bluegrass, fescue, or mixtures of these grasses, and will do well only if a continuous stream of fertilizer is applied.

Lawn fertilizers are composed of three elements: nitrogen, which keeps the grass dark green in color and increases top growth; phosphorus, which produces root growth and hastens the establishment of new seedlings; and potash, a catalyst in the food-production chain that also acts as a winter anti-freeze for the plant roots. The fertilizer grade or composition is the percentage numbers listed on the bag. For example, a bag reading 10-6-4 would be 10 percent nitrogen, 6 percent phosphorus and 4 percent potash. When applying the fertilizer, it is safe to assume that 5 pounds of fertilizer should be used per 1,000 square feet of lawn area.

These six simple rules will eliminate the hazards of fertilizing:

1. Buy the proper fertilizer for your needs—all fertilizers are different.
2. Do not overlap strips as this will cause over-fertilizing. Overlap wheels only.
3. Do not skip rows when fertilizing or yellowish streaks in the lawn will result.
4. Shut spreader off at all turns.
5. Do not refill the spreader on grass areas. A spill will burn the lawn.
6. Walk at an even pace so that you will not release too much or too little fertilizer.

Watering Grass roots need fresh air to survive and grow. Overwatering prevents the oxygen in the soil from being released, and the root system will rot, causing the plants to die. Underwatering can do as much damage because the roots will come closer to the surface to obtain water and will be dried out by the hot sun. Grass is approximately 85 percent water and will survive only if the roots can pull water from the surrounding soil.

A sprinkler is the most important element in keeping the soil moist. The type used is not as important as how it is used. Although a nozzle or hand-held sprinkler can be used, most people do not have the time or patience to saturate the entire lawn. The flat hose sprinkler (a hose with tiny holes in it) and oscillating sprinkler are more efficient and will cover small lawn areas effectively, but they must be moved periodically to ensure proper coverage. A flat hose can also be used on sloping areas.

The perfect solution is to have an underground system installed, which will efficiently water the lawn with little or no effort on your part. The system is initially expensive and should be installed by professionals to ensure that the sprinkler heads are properly located for complete coverage of the lawn. Most installers will give free construction and design estimates.

Traveling sprinklers are the best alternative to an underground system, especially on larger lawn areas. The sprinkler travels along the hose, which has been spread across the yard. It should be noted that one pass over the yard may not be enough, and it might be necessary to repeat the operation. Although it is the most expensive of the portable systems, it eliminates the aggravation of continuously moving the sprinkler to water the lawn.

The final type of sprinkler is the impulse or pulsator. This sprinkler is excellent for watering slopes and run-off areas because it delivers water slowly and affords good penetration of the soil. Oscillating sprinklers which finely mist the lawn are good for large areas.

Lawn-Care Calendar

Three lawn feedings each year—April, June, and September—and a regular maintenance program will achieve a green, thick, healthy lawn. The following month-by-month checklist should help you to care properly for your lawn.

March Rake the lawn completely if it is not soggy, wet, or frozen. Apply a fungicide to prevent turf diseases. Fungus will grow in wet turf when the temperature is between 35° and 100°, and the air is very muggy.

April April is an excellent month to seed. Cut the lawn to a height of 1½ inches. Rake off all clippings and other debris. Feed with a fertilizer that contains a pre-emergence crabgrass control, to prevent the sprouting of unwanted crabgrass, goose grass, and

the like. Both fertilizers may be applied separately, but this proves to be time consuming and serves no useful purpose. Also apply lime, allowing 25 pounds per 1,000 square feet.

May Continue cutting at a height of 1½ inches. Fertilize with a broadleaf weed killer to control nongrass weeds such as clover and plantain. The best time to eliminate broadleaf weeds is when they are actively growing.

June Raise cutting height to 2 inches. Water regularly but gently to avoid any puddling or run-off. The average lawn needs approximately 1½ inches of water per week (1 to 1½ hours of watering every other day) to maintain its lush green color and to produce its food. A lawn can be watered at any time of the day, although it is best to do so in the early morning hours. Wet grass and soil surfaces overnight might encourage the growth of a lawn fungus. Fertilize with a general purpose mixture of 10-6-4, 20-10-5, or 10-8-6. If you plan to apply a lawn insect controller, it should be done in early June, either separately or combined with a fertilizer.

July Continue cutting at a height of 2 inches. Increase watering to compensate for drier weather. If insect control was applied in June, repeat the application during the last week in July.

August Continue cutting and watering program.

September September also is an excellent month to seed. Fertilize with a general purpose fertilizer (see June), and continue cutting and watering program.

October Lower cutting height to 1½ inches. Apply lime if not done earlier in the year. Seed if not done in September. October is usually a very good month to thatch a lawn—remove matted dead grass and other lawn debris and aerate the soil. You may rent a thatching machine for this purpose or simply rake the lawn area thoroughly with a good metal rake, which is less efficient but will achieve almost the same results. After thatching, rake the lawn area. An average 10,000 square foot lawn would take approximately one full day to complete.

November Cut the lawn down to 1 inch before winter. Rake off all clippings and other debris. Feed with a fertilizer high in phosphorus and potash to protect the root system of the grass and to give it a quick start in the spring.

Lawn-Care Tips Your lawn-care monthly checklist can be more effective if you remember these five important rules:

1. Sharpen your mower blade frequently.
2. Always apply fertilizer and other dry products with a good mechanical spreader.
3. Water frequently during dry months.
4. Do not overapply fertilizers—follow directions.
5. Seek professional advice when problems arise that you feel need special attention.

How to Control Lawn Weeds and Diseases

Weeds

Lawn weeds are classified as either weed grasses or broadleaf weeds. Following are descriptions of the most troublesome weeds of each type and their treatments.

Weed Grasses Weed grasses resemble lawn grasses in structure but are generally more coarse, vary in color, and have visible seedheads. Most weed grasses can be pulled easily. Here are the more common varieties and the herbicides which are most effective on them:

- Crabgrass—This weed grass has thick stocks and a flat base; the seedheads are fanning, fingerlike projections. There are two types of treatment for crabgrass.

  In April or May, before seeds germinate, Dacthal or DSMA (disodium methanearsonate) is an excellent pretreatment, but apply only to a well-established lawn as this will retard the growth of new seedlings. One treatment usually gives complete control for the entire season. After applying, sprinkle lightly with water to wash the weed killer off the leaves into the soil.

  After the seeds have germinated, treat with two applications of good arsonate like DSMA or PMA (phenyl mercury acetate) at twelve- to fourteen-day intervals.

  To treat small patches of crabgrass, a solution of ¼ pound of Dalapon mixed with a gallon of water can be applied directly on the weed area with a spray applicator. If applied by hand, take special care to avoid contact with the skin. Cover all exposed body parts and wear rubber gloves.
- Bermuda Grass—Methyl bromide is by far the best substance to control this perennial grass because it requires only one application, but it releases gasses that are extremely lethal to man and animal. For this reason, it is not recommended unless applied by a professional. An effective and safer alternative is the use of Dalapon at a rate of ¼ pound per gallon of water. One gallon covers 1,000 square feet. Apply first from the middle to late June and repeat in about four weeks to kill any remaining plants.
- Nimble Will—This perennial weed grows in clumps of 10 inches or more. The leaf blades are short, and long stems house singular seeds. To control nimble Will, apply Siduron in the late fall or early spring.
- Foxtail—Foxtail is an annual weed grass that reproduces only by seeds. Yellow foxtail, the more common species, is a matlike plant with red stems at the base. Bristle is a longer variety with a bushy seedhead that looks somewhat like a cornhusk. Treatment is the same as for crabgrass.
- Goose Grass—This annual grass, which resembles crabgrass, will reproduce by seed. All blades grow from the center and remain rather flat or low to the ground. Although there is no completely effective method of control, it is commonly treated as a crabgrass.

Broadleaf Weeds The following common broadleaf weeds can be effectively controlled with 2,4-D (dichlorophenoxy acetic acid) or Silvex:

- Chickweed—Chickweed leaves are pointed and shiny. It is a low, spreading annual plant that will reproduce by seed or creeping stems that root themselves. The mouseear or hairy chickweed has elongated leaves covered with hairlike follicles. It is a perennial that produces usually by seed and only occasionally by rerooting.
- Clover—Clover is characterized by three separate leaflets joined together on a stem and by large white blossoms. Some people do not consider clover a weed and rather enjoy a minimal amount incorporated into their lawn, but it must be watched carefully before it gets out of hand and takes over completely.
- Dandelion—This deep-rooted plant which produces a bright yellow flower is probably the most recognized broadleaf weed. At the top of the stem are bushy, airlike seedpods that are easily dispersed by wind or animal intervention.
- Ground Ivy—A perennial that reproduces by seed or creeping stems, ground ivy is much like the climbing ivy in that all leaves are grown from a vine. Light purple flowers are produced in clusters at the junction of the stems and leaves. The vines will intertwine and smother out existing lawns.
- Henbit—Henbit has scalloped-shaped leaves that grow opposite each other on the stems. It is a slender annual that will grow 4 to 6 inches tall. Flowers are usually purple or pink.
- Sorrel—Yellow sorrel is a low-growing plant that reaches a height of up to 12 inches. The leaves are divided into heart-shaped leaflets on a long stalk; its flowers grow in clusters. Sheep sorrel grows more like the dandelion with a spear-shaped leaf. Both are perennial plants.
- Speedwell—The purslane variety has a fibrous root system and thick, rubbery leaves and stems. It produces a small white flower at the axil of the leaves and stem. Corn speedwell's notched, oval-shaped leaves and stem are covered with tiny hairs, and it produces a blue flower. Both varieties grow in the early spring.

Most lawn grasses are grown under cultivated conditions and are more subject to attack by disease organisms than they would be in their native environment. Healthy, vigorously growing, adapted lawn grasses that are properly managed best survive disease attacks.

The best defense against lawn diseases is to follow these basic principles of lawn establishment and maintenance:

- Select grasses adapted to the soil, climatic, and light conditions of your area.
- Spend the necessary time, effort, and money required to care for a lawn. In addition to disease control, lawn care includes proper fertilizing, watering, mowing, and insect/weed control.

Proper care does not completely prevent or cure diseases, but it helps to curb them so chemical controls can be more effective if they are needed.

Knowing how to diagnose the most common causes of dead or injured grass and knowing the recommended treatments for various unhealthy conditions will help prevent serious lawn damage. Poor turf may be due to disease or to any one or a combination of other causes—undesirable or unadapted variety of grass, insect damage, fertilizer and chemical burning, dog urine, improper mowing, improper watering, localized dry spots, and compacted soil.

Fungus Diseases

Fungi cause most of the serious and widespread diseases of lawn grasses. Most of the fungi that attack lawn grasses occur in the form of microscopically small filaments, or threads. The mass of threads, which sometimes have a cobwebby appearance, is called mycelium. Many fungi reproduce by means of microscopic fruiting structures called spores.

Only those fungi that get their nutrients from a living host are true disease organisms. Such organisms cause leafspot, fading-out, brown patch, rust, grease spot, dollar spot, stripe smut, and snow mold.

Mushrooms and slime molds in lawns are examples of fungi that are not true disease organisms. They do not attack lawn grasses directly but are discussed with disease organisms because they are a common, often unsightly, lawn problem.

Practices to Help Prevent Lawn Diseases

These practices are general guides. Their importance depends on the type and extent of the disease threat. Not all of them can be practiced under all conditions.

- Select grass species best adapted to the soil, climatic, and light conditions under which they will be grown.
- Plant mixtures of recommended grasses. Spe-

EFFECTIVENESS OF HERBICIDES FOR CONTROL OF COMMON LAWN WEEDS

Weed	Type of Plant	Control[1]		
		2,4-D	MCPA	Silvex
Bindweed, field (Convolvulus arvensis)	Perennial	Good	Good	Good
Buttercup, creeping (Ranunculus repens)	Perennial	Very good	Excellent	Excellent
Chickweed, common (Stellaria media)	Annual	Good	Fair	Excellent
Chickweed, mouseear (Cerastium vulgatum)	Perennial	Good	Fair	Excellent
Cinquefoil, Canada (Potentilla canadensis)	Perennial	Very good	Good	Good
Cinquefoil, sulphur (Potentilla recta)	Perennial	Very good	Good	Good
Dandelion (Taraxacum officinale)	Perennial	Excellent	Excellent	Excellent
Dock, curly (Rumex crispus)	Perennial	Very good	Good	Fair
Garlic, wild (Allium vineale)	Perennial	Good	Fair	Poor
Goose grass (Eleusine indica)	Annual	Poor	Poor	Poor
Ground ivy (Glecoma hederacea)	Perennial	Good	Fair	Very good
Henbit (Lamium amplexicaule)	Annual	Fair	Fair	Very good
Ivy, English (Hedera helix)	Perennial			
Knawel, annual (Scleranthus annuus)	Annual	Poor	Poor	Good
Knotweed (Polygonum aviculare)	Annual	Good	Fair	Good
Medic, black (Medicago lupulina)	Annual	Good	Good	Very good
Moneywort (Lysimachia nummularia)	Perennial	Excellent		
Nutsedge, purple (Cyperus rotundus)	Perennial	Fair	Poor	Poor
Nutsedge, yellow (Cyperus esculentus)	Perennial	Fair	Poor	Poor
Pennywort, lawn (Hydrocotyle rotundifolia)	Perennial	Very good		Excellent
Plantain, broadleaf (Plantago major)	Perennial	Excellent	Excellent	Very good
Plantain, buckhorn (Plantago lanceolata)	Perennial	Excellent	Very good	Very good
Plantain, rugel (Plantago rugelii)	Perennial	Excellent	Excellent	Very good
Poison ivy (Rhus radicans)	Woody	Good	Good	Excellent
Poison oak (Rhus diversiloba)	Woody	Good	Fair	Excellent
Puncturevine (Tribulus terrestris)	Annual	Very good	Fair	
Sorrel, red (Rumex acetosella)	Perennial	Poor	Poor	Fair
Speedwell, corn (Veronica arvensis)	Annual	Fair	Poor	Fair
Speedwell purslane (Veronica peregrina)	Annual	Good	Poor	
Spurge, spotted (Euphorbia maculata)	Annual	Fair		Good
Strawberry, wild (Fragaria)	Perennial	Fair	Poor	Good
Thistle, Canada (Cirsium arvense)	Perennial	Good	Good	Good
Violet (Viola)	Perennial	Fair	Poor	Good
Woodsorrel, yellow (Oxalis stricta)	Perennial	Fair	Poor	Very good

[1]Omission of a term indicates effectiveness is not known.
Source: U.S. Department of Agriculture.

GUIDE FOR SELECTING FUNGICIDES

Disease	Fungicides	Application per 1,000 sq. ft.		Directions
		Ounces of Formulation	Tablespoons	
Brown Patch	Cleary's 3336® WP 50%	2	11	Disease can appear from June to August. Treat your lawn every 7 to 10 days until the disease has been controlled.
	Daconil 2787® WP 75%	4	22	
	Dyrene® WP 50%	4 to 6	19 to 28	
	Fore® WP 80%	4	14	
	Fungo 50® WP 50%	2	11	
	Mertect 140—F® liquid	2	4	
	Tersan 1991® WP 50%	2	11	
	Tersan LSR® WP 80%	6	4 to 5	
Copper Spot	See Dollar Spot			
Dollar Spot	Acti-dione-Thiram® WP	2 to 4	11 to 22	Disease can appear from June to October. Treat your lawn at 7 to 10 day intervals until the disease has been controlled.
	Cleary's 3336® WP 50%	2	11	
	Daconil 2787® WP 75%	2 to 4	11 to 22	
	Dyrene® WP 50%	4 to 6	19 to 28	
	Tersen 1991® WP 50%	2	11	
	Fore® WP 80%	6 to 8	14 to 21	
	Fungo 50® WP 50%	1	6	
	Mertect 140—F® liquid	2	4	
Fairy Rings Mushrooms	Captan WP 50%	4 to 5	15 to 20	Disease can appear throughout the growing season. Pour double- or triple-strength concentrate of Captan into 1-inch holes punched 4 to 6 inches deep and 6 to 8 inches apart both inside and outside the affected area.
	Dowfume MC-2			
Fusarium Blight	Cleary's 3336® WP 50%	4 to 8	11 to 22	Treat at first appearance of disease and repeat 7 to 10 days later. Water thoroughly to wet into soil.
	Fungo 50® WP 50%	4 to 8	19 to 38	
	Tersan 1991® WP 50%	2	33	
Grease Spot and Cottony Blight	Tersan SP® WP 65%	4	5 to 6	Disease can appear from July to September and in fall and winter during warm, humid periods in the South. Treat your lawn every 5 to 14 days until the disease has been controlled.
	Dexon® WP 70%	2	14	
	Fore® WP 80%	8	28	
	Koban® WP 65%	4	17	
	Zineb WP 75%	2	13 to 27	
Helminthosporium Diseases Leafspot (Blight, Going-out, Melting-out)	Acti-dione-Thiram® WP	4	22	Disease can appear from April to August, depending on kind of grass and species of fungus. Treat your lawn every 7 to 10 days three times consecutively or until the disease has been controlled.
	Captan WP 50%	4 to 6	15 to 23	
	Cleary's 3336® WP 50%	2	11	
	Daconil 2787® WP 75%	4	22	
	Dyrene® WP 50%	4 to 6	19 to 28	
	Fore® WP 80%	4	14	
	Tersan LSR® WP 80%	3 to 4	4 to 5	
	Zineb WP 75%	2	13 to 27	
Powdery Mildew	Acti-dione Thiram®	4	22	July to September
	Acti-dione TGF® WP	1 to 2	6	7 to 10 days
	Tersan 1991® WP 50%	2	11	7 to 14 days
Red Thread	Acti-dione Thiram® WP	4	22	May, June, and August, every 10 to 14 days.
	Cleary's 3336® WP 50%	2	11	
	Fore® WP 80%	4 to 6	14 to 21	
	Fungo 50® WP 50%	2	11	
	Tersan LSR® WP 80%	6	4 to 5	
Rust	Acti-dione-Thiram® WP	4	22	Disease can appear from June to September. Treat your lawn every 7 to 14 days until rust disappears.
	Daconil 2787® WP 75%	4	22	
	Dyrene® WP 50%	4 to 6	19 to 28	
	Fore® WP 80%	4	14	
	Tersan LSR® WP 80%	3 to 4	4 to 5	
	Zineb WP 75%	2	13 to 27	
Slime Molds	Fore® WP 80%	6 to 8	21 to 28	Disease can appear throughout the growing season and can be controlled without fungicides.
	Zineb WP 75%	2	13 to 27	

Disease	Product			Directions
Snow Molds Fusarium Patch	Tersan 1991® WP 50%	2	11	Disease can appear from fall to spring. Treat your lawn at intervals of 2 to 6 weeks as needed.
	Mertect 140—F® liquid	2	2	
	Fore® WP 80%	6 to 8	21 to 28	
	Fungo 50® WP 50%	2	11	
Typhula Blight	Tersan SP® WP 65%	6 to 8	5 to 6	Disease can appear from fall to spring. Treat your lawn at intervals of 2 to 6 weeks as needed.
	Dyrene WP 50%	2 to 3	19 to 28	
Stripe Smut	Fungo 50® WP 50%	4 to 8	19 to 38	One application in October or early spring before grass growth begins. Water thoroughly to wet into soil.
	Tersan 1991® WP 50%	6	33	

CAUTION: Do not graze treated areas or feed clippings to livestock.
*The directions given in the above table may not be complete enough. Be sure to read and follow the manufacturer's directions for all fungicide applications.

cies vary in their susceptibility to different disease organisms, and in a mixture one or more of the grasses usually will survive a severe disease attack.

- Do not clip upright-growing grasses such as Kentucky bluegrass and red fescue too closely—1¾ to 2 inches is the best height. Creeping grasses such as bent grass and zoysia may be clipped at ½ inch or less.
- Mow the grass before it gets too tall; not more than one-half of the leaf surface should be removed at one time.
- Mow the lawn frequently enough in the fall to prevent the accumulation of a thick mat of grass before snow comes.
- Apply enough fertilizer to keep grass vigorously growing but avoid overstimulating the grass with nitrogen. Apply lime if soil tests indicate a need for it.
- Clippings need not be removed except on heavily fertilized lawns or during periods when the grass is growing rapidly. Clippings provide nutrients for fungi and help to maintain humidity long after the sun has dried off surrounding uncovered areas.
- Water early enough in the day to allow grass leaves time to dry out before night. Avoid frequent, light waterings, especially during warm weather.
- Do not water grass until it begins to wilt, then soak the soil to a depth of 6 inches or more. Provide good surface drainage.

Other Causes of Poor Turf

Undesirable Species Short-lived perennials like red-top and ryegrass or weedy annuals such as annual bluegrass and crabgrass do not make a desirable lawn. Annual species usually die at the end of the growing season and leave brown or bare areas that may be mistaken for disease injury.

Undesirable Mixtures Bermuda grasses and zoysia grasses turn straw colored or brown following a killing frost. When these species are grown in a sod composed mainly of cool-season grasses, a mottled brown and green lawn often results because of the differences in sensitivity to cold. This effect may resemble disease injury.

Insect Injury Lawn grasses are often damaged by insect pests. For information concerning lawn insects and their control, see the following chapter, contact your county agent, or write to the U.S. Department of Agriculture, Washington, D.C. 20250.

Fertilizer Burn Concentrated inorganic fertilizers, if applied too heavily, burn grass in two or three days. Burned areas may occur in spots or streaks, or the entire lawn may be damaged. To prevent injury, apply the fertilizer evenly in recommended amounts when the grass is dry, then water immediately. If burning occurs, water generously to wash off excess fertilizer and reduce injury.

Hydrated Lime Burn Hydrated lime burns grass if it is applied unevenly and in large amounts. Ground agricultural limestone is safer and is usually recommended for lawns.

Pesticide Injury Some of the chemicals used for disease, insect, and weed control are potent and may injure grass if improperly applied. Chemical formulations vary with manufacturers. Carefully follow directions and observe all precautions on the label.

Dog Urine Injury This kind of injury is frequently mistaken for disease damage. Affected spots are usually round or slightly irregular and variable in size. The grass within the spot turns brown or straw colored and usually dies.

Improper Mowing Cutting grass too closely or too frequently may result in a condition that looks like disease. Cut Kentucky bluegrass, red fescue, and other grasses with upright growth habit to a height of 1¼ to 2 inches. Do not lower the height of cutting in midseason; it may result in serious injury. Mow the grass before it gets too tall; not more than one-half of the leaf surface should be removed at one time. Clippings need not be removed unless growth is excessive.

Improper Watering Frequent light watering induces shallow rooting in grasses. Shallow-rooted grasses are readily injured during periods of severe drought. Frequent evening watering favors disease development because it keeps grass leaves moist for long periods.

Do not water grass until it begins to wilt, then apply enough water to soak the soil to a depth of 6 inches or more. It is more economical to water the lawn only when water is needed, and it is better for the grass.

Buried Debris A thin layer of soil over rocks or debris such as lumber, stumps, plaster, and cement dries rapidly and may not retain enough moisture to keep grass green. Correct this condition by removing the cause.

Accumulation of Runners Another type of dry spot results when an accumulation of runners (thatch) in Bermuda grass, bent grass, and zoysia grass becomes impervious and does not let water into the soil. Mowing following vigorous hand raking corrects this condition.

Compacted Soils Saturated soils pack easily and bake hard when dry, especially where traffic is heavy. The soil may become packed so hard that water will not penetrate the surface. Grass then thins out, and bare spots result. To correct this condition, loosen or perforate the soil with a tined fork or aerifying implement and, if necessary, fertilize and reseed the lawn.

How to Control Lawn Insects

Many insects and insectlike pests damage lawns and other turf. They cause the grass to turn brown and die, or they build unsightly mounds that may smother the grass. Some pests infest the soil and attack plant roots; some feed on leaves and stems; others suck juice from the plants. Some insects and pests inhabit lawns but do not damage them. But these pests may be annoying and can be controlled with insecticides.

Pests That Infect Soil and Roots

Grubs Grubs are the larval stage of various beetles. They are white or gray, with brown heads and brown or black hind parts. Grubs generally measure 1 to 1½ inches and are usually found in a curled position. They hatch from eggs laid in the ground by the female beetles. Most spend about ten months of the year in the ground; some remain in the soil two or three years. In mild weather, they live 1 to 3 inches below the surface of the lawn; in winter, they go deeper into the soil below the frost line. Grubs feed on the roots of grass plants about 1 inch below the surface. Moles, skunks, and birds feed on the grubs and may tear up the sod searching for them. Grubs can damage turf in either spring or fall.

Treat with Diazinon. In infested areas, applications should be repeated every two weeks. If large areas have been damaged by the grub, it will be necessary to remove the dead sod, level the ground with fresh loam, and reseed.

Common beetles and grubs include:

- May Beetles—brown or blackish brown beetles, commonly called June beetles. They are most numerous in June but can appear as early as April in the South and as late as August in the Southwest. The young are called white grubs. Some remain in the soil two or three years and may feed on the grass roots during several seasons.
- Japanese Beetles—about ½ inch long with a shiny metallic-green body; it has coppery-brown wings and six small patches of white hairs along each side and the back of the body, just under the edges of the wings. The adult insect feeds on many plant species. The insects appear in late May or June and are active four to six weeks.
- Asiatic Garden Beetles—chestnut brown, about ¼ inch long and velvety in appearance. The underside of the body is covered with short yellow hairs. The insect flies only at night and feeds on various kinds of foliage. These beetles are most abundant in widely scattered places along the Atlantic seaboard from mid-July to mid-August.
- Oriental Beetles—about ⅝ inch long, straw colored, and some dark markings on the body. They appear in the New England area in late June, July, and August. The grubs prefer unshaded lawn and short grass.
- European Chafers—about ½ inch long and light chocolate brown or tan. The insects emerge from the soil at dusk, swarm into the trees and shrubs, and make a buzzing sound. The beetles appear in June and July and are most abundant in early July.

- Masked Chafers—½ inch long and brown. They live in the soil during the day and emerge at night. They are especially active on warm humid evenings. The northern masked chafer is found from Connecticut south to Alabama and west to California. The southern masked chafer is common in the southeastern states. Masked chafers appear in late June and July and are active one or two months. The young are sometimes called annual white grubs because the life cycle is completed in one year.
- Rose Chafers—½ inch long and yellowish brown with long spiny legs. Rose chafers feed on almost any vegetation and are very destructive to roses in bloom. They thrive in light and sandy soils. The insects are found in eastern United States and west to Colorado and Texas in June and early July.
- Green June Beetles—nearly 1 inch long, bodies are somewhat flattened, velvety green with bronze to yellow edges. The females often lay eggs in piles of grass clippings as well as in the soil. Green June beetles are found mostly in southern regions. They are active in June, July, and August and produce one generation a year. The grubs feed mainly on decaying vegetable matter. Damage is most severe in dry seasons and is most apparent in the fall. These grubs have the unusual habit of crawling on their backs. Areas damaged by grubs appear brown and cracked and can be rolled back like a carpet. When testing, take a piece of damaged sod and flip it over. If grubs are present you will be able to see them on the underside among the roots of the plant.

Other Burrowing Pests Several other insects and pests can directly or indirectly damage lawns. They include:

- Ants—build nests in the ground that can smother the surrounding grass. If the ants nest in the roots of the grass, they may destroy them. Ants also destroy grass seeds in the ground and prevent good stands.
- Mole Crickets—are light brown. Their lower surface is lighter than the upper and is often tinged with green. They are about 1½ inches long. Mole crickets feed on the roots of the grass and their burrowing uproots seedlings and causes the soil to dry out quickly. One mole cricket can damage several yards of a newly seeded lawn in a single night. These insects are most numerous in the South Atlantic and Gulf Coast states.
- Wireworms—which are the larvae of click beetles are ½ to 1½ inches long and are usually hard, dark brown, smooth, and slender. Some are soft and white or yellow. Wireworms bore into the underground part of the stems and feed on grass roots. Boring generally kills the plant. Adults are hard shelled and their bodies taper somewhat at each end.
- Cicada-Killer Wasps—are about 1½ inches long and have yellow and black body markings. The wasps dig deep nests in the ground and mound the soil at the entrance to the nests. These wasps appear in late July and August in the eastern United States.
- Wild Bees—can damage lawns by digging up the soil, making holes, and forming mounds that interfere with the growth of grass.
- Periodical Cicadas—nymphs leave many small holes in lawns, especially under trees. If you hear the day-long song of the cicada in the spring of a year in which a brood is scheduled to appear in your region, the holes in your lawn have probably been made by the emerging nymphs. If a large brood is emerging, protect ornamental trees and shrubs.
- Billbugs—grubs are small and white, and have hard brown or yellow heads. They feed on grass roots. Adult billbugs are beetles ⅕ to ¾ inch long. They have long snouts and are clay yellow to reddish brown to jet black. The beetles burrow in the grass stems near the surface of the soil and also feed on the leaves.

Pests That Feed on Leaves and Stems

Sod Webworms Sod webworms are about ¾ inch long and light brown. Their bodies are covered with fine hairs. Sod webworms are the larvae of lawn moths which are small, white, or gray moths (or millers). They hide in the shrubbery or other sheltered spots during the day. In the early evening, they fly over the grass, and the females scatter eggs over the lawns. Worms emerge in six to ten days and work only at night. As soon as they are hatched, the larvae start feeding on the grass leaves. As they grow larger, they build burrows or tunnels close to the surface of the soil. Some species feed on the grass crowns at ground level and on the roots.

Several species infest lawns. The tropical sod webworm is the most important one in Florida. The burrowing sod webworm infests lawn grasses from Kansas south to Louisiana and east to Maryland. You can find the worms by breaking apart some of the dying sod. Sod webworms prefer new lawns. Grass blades are often cut in half, and sometimes the entire plant is severed at the crown. Irregular brown spots are the first signs of damage. The foliage becomes stripped in patches, leaving a yellow-brown appearance similar to drought. Because sod webworms remain hidden during the day, the best method of identification is to watch for the adult moths flying over the lawn at dusk.

Extensive damage may require reseeding. Control with liquid Diazinon. Treatment should start as soon as damage is noticed and should be repeated every six weeks through September. An insect controller can be applied during regular seasonal maintenance as a preventative measure.

Other Leaf-Foraging Pests Several insects and their larvae can cause severe damage to leaves and stems. Most can be controlled with a pesticide. They include:

- Armyworms—are the larvae of moths. They are 1½ inches long, with green and black stripes along each side and down the center of the back. Adults are brownish gray; their wings measure about 1½ inches across when expanded. They may devour the grass down to the ground when numerous. Their feeding causes circular bare areas in lawns.
- Cutworms—are dull-brown, gray, or nearly black caterpillars and are 1½ to 2 inches long. Some cutworms are spotted, others striped. They usually hide in the soil during the day and feed at night. They are the larvae of night-flying brown or gray moths. Cutworms infest lawns and feed on the leaves or cut off the grass near the soil. They may do severe damage to seedlings of Bermuda grass, bent grass, and ryegrass.
- Fiery Skipper—larvae feed on the leaves of common lawn grasses but attack bent grass most severely. Early infestation is indicated by isolated, round bare spots, 1 to 2 inches in diameter. The adults are small, yellowish-brown butterflies.
- Lucerne Moth—larvae prefer clover and other legumes but also infest grass. The adult is a grayish-brown moth with two pairs of dark spots on each forewing.
- Leaf Bugs—feed on lawns causing the grass to die out in spots. These gray and white insects attack bluegrass, Bermuda grass, and bent grass throughout the United States.
- Frit Flies—are present in a number of states across the country. The adult fly is black and about ¹⁄₁₆ inch long. The female lays eggs on the grass, and the hatching maggots bore into the stems.

Pests That Suck Plant Juice

Chinch Bugs Most chinch bug damage is caused by the young bugs, or nymphs. Nymphs hatch from eggs laid by the female adults. Females can lay as many as 600 eggs per month. At first a nymph is about half the size of a pinhead; it is bright red and has a white band across the back. The full-grown nymph is black and has a white spot on the back between the wing pads. The adults are about ¹⁄₁₆ inch long; they are black and have white markings.

The first sign of chinch bugs may be mistaken for drought. Patches of dead grass appear in areas where heat is radiated, often along sidewalks or driveways. A brown spot that spreads in a wavelike fashion may also appear on the lawn. To test for chinch bugs, remove both ends of a metal coffee can and press it into the ground next to the damaged area. Fill the can with water. If the bugs are present, they will float to the surface.

Chinch bugs kill grasses by injecting a toxin into the plant. A damaged area will not revive itself and must be reseeded.

Chinch bugs can be controlled with liquid Diazinon or with the granular mixes marked for insect control, which should be applied immediately once damage is noticed and repeated every six weeks through September. As a safeguard, an insect control plus fertilizer can be applied during your regular seasonal maintenance.

Other Related Pests Several other insects can damage lawns by sucking juices from the tender grass leaves.

- False chinch bugs—are frequently mistaken for chinch bugs. They feed on grasses but are rarely lawn pests. The nymphs are greenish gray; the adults are gray.
- Scale insects—suck juice from grasses; some feed on the crown of the plants and above-ground parts; others feed on the roots. The grass becomes yellow, then brown, and finally dies. Damage is usually more severe in dry periods. Several kinds of scales damage lawns in the southern part of the United States. No satisfactory way has been found to control scales on lawns. Consult your county agricultural agent or state agricultural experiment station for current recommendations.
- Leafhoppers—are tiny triangular or wedge-shaped insects that fly or hop short distances. They are less than ⅕ inch long and are green, yellow, or brownish gray. They suck the sap from the leaves and stems of the grass. New lawns may be damaged so extensively that reseeding is necessary. Damage to established lawns is evident in whitened patches.
- Mites—Several species of mites attack grasses. They suck the sap and cause the leaves to be blotched and stippled. They are not ordinarily pests in well-managed lawns, but severe infestations can kill the plants.
- Spittlebugs—seldom damage well-managed lawns. The nymphs live inside spittle masses and suck juices from plants. The adults resemble leafhoppers in appearance and habits. Control measures in lawns are seldom necessary.

Pests That Inhabit but Do Not Damage Lawns

Several insects and pests may be present in your lawn without causing damage to grass plants. Their presence, however, can be annoying to people and pets because of their bite. These pests include: mosquitoes, earwigs, ticks, chiggers, spiders, slugs or snails, centipedes, millipedes, sowbugs, and fleas. Some of these insects, such as some species of spiders, are actually helpful because they devour harmful pests.

Pesticides

The all-encompassing term pesticides refers to insecticides (used to control insects), fungicides (used to control fungus), and herbicides (used to control weeds).

Pesticides are available in many formulations under several trade names. Pesticides can be purchased in two forms, granular or spray, which includes the dusts. For a spray, powders are usually mixed with an emulsifier (spray solution) or water and applied with a compressed-air sprayer. Many of the pesticides in dust form can be bought ready to use. Although dusts and sprays are equally effective, the latter are preferred because they adhere to the plants' surfaces more readily.

As a rule of thumb, sprays are applied at a rate of one quart per 100 square feet of area. In gardens the rate decreases to one quart per 50-foot row. Dusts are applied at a rate of one ounce per 75 feet of area or in gardens, one ounce per 30- to 35-foot row. Granular forms are applied with a spreader according to the application instructions on the package.

Insecticides Insecticides are both stomach and contact poisons. They are classified by their composition—usually as organic, phosphorus or chlorinated hydrocarbons. Carbamate insecticides, in the hydrocarbon group, are used on a wide range of insects. While not harmful to man, they can harm some species of warm-blooded animals. The phosphate group provides the greatest protection against mites on fruit trees and vegetables but are extremely dangerous to man. Caution should be taken when applying phosphates.

Controlling soil insects can be difficult; therefore it is important to apply the insecticide at the time of year when the insect is most susceptible to control. This information is generally printed on the label.

To control underground lawn pests, apply the proper insecticide (see following table) and immediately sprinkle the lawn thoroughly. It may take a month or longer for the insecticide to become fully effective.

To control above-ground lawn pests apply the ap-

LAWN PESTS AND INSECTICIDES TO USE IN THEIR CONTROL[1]

Lawn pest	Diazinon (Spectracide)	Carbaryl (Sevin)	Chloropyrifos (Dursban)	Trichlorofon (Dylox)
Ants[2]	X	X	X	
Armyworms	X	X	X	X
Billbugs	X	X		
Chiggers	X		X	
Chinch bugs	X	X	X	
Cicada-killer wasps	X			
Cutworms[3]	X	X	X	X
Earwigs	X	X	X	
Fleas	X	X	X	
Frit fly	X			
Grasshopper			X	
Grubs[4]	X		X	X
Leafhopper	X	X		
Millipeds	X	X		
Clover mites	X		X	
Sod webworm	X	X	X	X
Ticks	X		X	

[1] Several insects are not listed either because no control measures are necessary or chemicals for their control are not registered at this time.

[2] If only a few ant nests are present, treat them individually. Wash the insecticide into the nests or drench the mounds with it. Special treatment is required to control fire and harvester ants; consult your State Agricultural Experiment Station for latest recommendations.

[3] To control cutworms, apply the insecticide in late afternoon.

[4] In hot, dry areas, lower dosages may be necessary to prevent burning the grass; consult your State Agricultural Experiment Station.

propriate insecticide to the grass. Sprinkle lightly to wash the insecticide into the crowns of the plants. Repeat the application when necessary.

Fungicides Fungicides are used to combat tiny organisms (fungi) that lack chlorophyll to manufacture their own food and must rely on other living or dead matter to survive.

Inorganic fungicides contain mercury compounds and a sulfur-lime combination. If used as a part of your yearly lawn maintenance program, they are effective against fungus such as scab or brown rot, which will grow on damp lawns during periods of excessive moisture.

Organic fungicides are generally synthetic compounds used to kill rust and fungus on ornamentals, shrubs, fruit trees, and vegetables. Commonly used mixtures are Maneb, for leaf spots (dark spots that cover the leaves); Zineb, for rust (a brown substance that covers stems and leaves); and Phaltan, for mildew (a gray, powdery substance that covers leaves). These fungicides should be first applied during the peak months for fungus growth—April, May, and June— and repeated every two weeks. Careful application is necessary to ensure complete coverage of the plant; otherwise the fungus will continue to grow on parts that are left exposed.

Special Precautions Store pesticides in original containers out of reach of children and pets and away from food.

Apply pesticides selectively and carefully. Do not apply a pesticide when there is danger of drift to other areas. Avoid prolonged inhalation of a pesticide spray or dust. When applying a pesticide be fully clothed to avoid body contact with the mixture. Do not apply insecticides to a lawn when people or animals are present, and do not permit children and pets on the lawn until the insecticide has been washed off by sprinkling and the grass has dried completely.

After handling a pesticide, do not eat, drink, or smoke until you have washed. If a pesticide is swallowed or gets in the eyes, follow the first aid treatment given on the label and get prompt medical attention. If a pesticide is spilled on your skin or clothing, remove clothing immediately and wash skin thoroughly. Dispose of empty pesticide containers by wrapping them in several layers of newspaper and placing them in your trash can.

It is difficult to remove all traces of a herbicide (weed killer) from equipment. Therefore, to prevent injury to desirable plants, do not use the same equipment for insecticides and fungicides that you use for a herbicide.

Gardening Tools and Equipment

Perhaps the earliest sign of spring is the appearance of new garden tools and equipment in department stores and nurseries and in advertisements. These displays can both tempt and bewilder the beginning gardener. Yet the selection of the proper tools for each task is an important first step on the path to successful landscaping.

A project that should be simple and enjoyable can be made difficult and frustrating by the absence of a needed tool, so plan ahead to avoid interrupting your yard work with time-consuming trips to the garden center. Keep in mind that tools can be a costly investment. Purchase only those that you will need and use often, and plan to spend a little extra for the best quality. With proper care, they will give you years of service. Before purchasing any tool inspect it carefully. Lift and practice the motion used for the tool to be sure it is the proper weight and size for you. Tools which feel right will make landscaping much easier.

In this chapter we will describe the hand and power tools that you should purchase or rent and suggest techniques for storing and maintaining your landscaping equipment.

Hand Tools

Lawn and Leaf Rake Two types are available—metal and bamboo. Although they both do a thorough job, the metal type is sturdier. This valuable tool is used for raking light matter, such as leaves or grass clippings.

Grass-Trimming Shears For a professional touch, use hand shears to trim along walks, flower beds, and driveways. Select shears that can be easily taken apart for sharpening and cleaning.

Drop-Action Spreader Standard models come in 18-, 22-, and 24-inch widths and are essential for seeding, fertilizing, and liming your lawn. Broadcast spreaders are ideal for fertilizing and seeding your lawn. They will cut your time in half, but are not recommended for liming.

Half-Moon Edger This tool penetrates sod quickly for easy removal and keeps a straight edge along beds.

Square-Bladed Spade or Square Shovel This tool is a must for pile pickup and root pruning.

Pitchfork Use this tool for turning over soil, preparing seed beds, or removing loosened sod. Short-handled forks generally work best in crowded areas.

Steel Straight Head Rake This tool, similar to the bow rake, is used to rough-rake and level the ground. Although not necessary for the beginner, it is useful when leveling in order to eliminate small shoots such as weeds and grass that are mixed with the soil.

Long-Handled Pointed Shovel Digging holes for plantings is mainly done with this tool.

Pruning Shears This valuable aid is used for pruning small branches without bruising them or for cutting flowers for the table.

Hedge Shears Hedges, light growth, or ground cover can be pruned or shaped quickly and easily to give them a professional look. This shears is not meant for cutting thick branches. Pick a pair that can be taken apart for sharpening or cleaning.

Lopping Shears These long-handled and sturdy shears are used to prune bothersome branches that are up to 1½ inches in diameter.

Pruning Saw This saw cuts hard-to-get-at branches and limbs that are over 1½ inches in diameter.

Hand Tool Set This set consists of a small hoe, trowel, and cultivator that can be used for grooming flower beds. They serve a variety of important functions, such as weeding, making furrows, breaking up large soil clods, and bulb planting, to mention just a few.

Garden Hoes There are hoes for almost any type of landscaping or gardening job. The most common variety, with a 6-inch wide blade, is used primarily for chopping and grading.

Garden Hose A 50-foot hose is a good workable length. A vinyl hose is just as effective as the more expensive rubber hose and, if maintained properly, will last almost as long. A ⅝- or ½-inch inside diameter will give sufficient water pressure.

Larger Tools

Most of the rental shops carry all the tools that you will need. Before you invest in the larger tools, such as a wheelbarrow, roller, spreader, or rototiller, it would be wise to rent them and decide if they would be used enough to warrant their purchase.

Select rental tools as carefully as you would if buying them. Your whole purpose in renting a tool is to save you time and energy, which will be wasted if you have to return it for repairs or replacement. Here are a few things to look for when you rent or buy a larger tool.

Wheelbarrow Make sure that a wheelbarrow is clean and not rusted. Also check the pneumatic or hard rubber wheel to make sure it will stand up to the weight of a heavy load.

Spreader Make sure that the controls on a spreader work properly and that the discharge chute is not rusted.

Roller Make sure that there are no large dents in the drum of a roller, which would make contact with the soil impossible.

Rototiller Make sure that a rototiller starts easily, that all controls work properly, and that the blades are not bent or damaged.

Lawn Mowers

The lawn mower is the most essential power tool. To select the model best suited to your needs, consult your local dealer, who will recommend the proper size and horsepower for the area to be cut and the use of the mower. A rotary-type mower that is too heavy can compact the soil and squeeze out the vital air that is needed for your grass to survive. The Hahn or Toro mowers are recommended for their efficiency and weight, but they are fairly expensive. A push-type mower should be light and have tempered steel blades that will remain sharper longer. A sit-down or rider mower, because of its weight, is recommended for use only on larger lawn areas where nothing else is practical. The light and easily maneuvered electric mower is an excellent machine for smaller lawns that are cut frequently. However, the narrow cutting width and restricting cord make the electric mower impractical for use on large or heavily treed areas. The chart outlines the characteristics of the various types of mowers.

All mower manufacturers provide operating manuals that should be carefully read to ensure safety. Follow these common-sense rules:

1. Keep children far away from mowing area, and never direct the discharge chute toward any bystanders.
2. Wear good heavy shoes and long pants while operating your mower, to protect your feet and legs.
3. Never cut in the rain or when the grass is wet. You may injure yourself and damage the lawn by pulling and tearing the grass.
4. Mow only during the daylight hours when you can see what you are cutting and are less apt to strike an object.
5. Always stop the engine when you leave the machine for any reason.
6. Never fill the gas tank on a lawn because spilled gas will kill the grass. Also never refill a gas tank when it is hot from running.
7. If you strike an object, stop the mower and disconnect the spark plug wire; then replace or fix any damaged part before operating again.

Electric Hedge or Grass Clippers Although there are many other power tools available, a lawn mower and hedge clippers are probably the only ones necessary at the beginning stages of home landscaping. Electric grass trimmers are also a popular time- and work-conserving tool. Electric hedge clippers will save you time but can be very dangerous if not used properly. Read the owner's manual before operating and observe these cautions:

1. Always cut with the cord safely behind you.
2. Keep both hands on the handles.
3. Never cut while off balance or stretching.

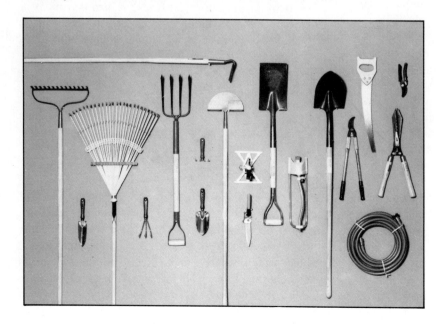

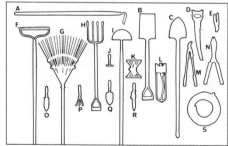

(A) hoe, (B) square-bladed spade, (C) long-handled pointed shovel, (D) pruning saw, (E) pruning shears, (F) steel rake, (G) lawn and leaf rake, (H) pitchfork, (I) half moon edger, (J) hand cultivator, (K) impact sprinkler, (L) oscillating sprinkler, (M) lopping shears, (N) hedge shears, (O, P, and Q) various hand tools, (R) grass-trimming shears, (S) hose.

COMPARISON OF LAWN MOWERS

Mower	Lot Size in Thousand Sq. Ft.	Size Mower in Inches	Average Cost per Hour	Comments
Rotary (Push Type) 3-4 Horsepower	10-15	19-22	$.25	Easy to handle in tight areas.
Rotary (Power Driven) 3-4 Horsepower	10-25	19-22	.30	Excellent for straight areas. Difficult to handle in close quarters.
Reel (Push Type)	up to 5	19-20	—	Usually needs second cut to be effective. Blades need constant sharpening.
Reel (Power Driven) 3-4 Horsepower	5-15	19-20	.25	Blades must be adjusted and sharpened constantly.
Sit Down 4-7 Horsepower	over 25	20-40	.50	Will compact soil—use only when essential.
Electric	up to 10	16-20	.13	Cord is a bother and expensive to replace. Efficient except around flower beds where cord gets in the way.

4. If you should cut the cord, it will give a minor shock. Immediately shut off the clippers, disconnect them, and repair the damage before resuming the cutting.

Remember, all power tools are safely made—it is the careless person who makes them unsafe.

Care of Tools

Every time you use a garden tool, you should clean and oil it. A cleaning box is extremely helpful for this task. One can be easily made by building a box about 2 feet square and 1 foot high. Fill the box with sand that has been saturated with motor oil. After you have completed your job in the garden, simply push your tool into the cleaning box several times. The sand will remove the soil and chemicals, while the oil lubricates the tool to prevent rusting. Although aluminum tools do not rust, this treatment will help to prevent pitting.

Generally, the handles will break or wear out long before the tool itself. They can usually be replaced at a fraction of the price of a new tool. Check your local hardware store or garden center to find the proper replacement handle.

Sharpening Blades Push mowers and electric hedge clippers should be sharpened by a mower service man, but a rotary mower blade can be sharpened with a large heavy-duty mill file. First disconnect the spark plug wire. Tip the mower on its side with the carburetor facing upward to minimize gas spills. Turn the holding screw in a counterclockwise direction to remove the blade, and place it in a vise so that only one cutting edge is exposed. Take the file in both hands and lay it across the blade following the counter of the beveled edge (the slant of the cutting edge). Starting from the inside of the blade and applying slightly more pressure on the lower hand, push the file toward the end of the blade.

Repeat this several times until you have a sharp edge. Now turn the blade over and follow the same steps for the other cutting edge.

After the blade has been sharpened, make sure that it is balanced by placing a round rod through the blade's center hole. If the blade lays straight across the rod, it is balanced. If it should dip slightly, refile one or both sides until it is balanced.

Grass shears, hedge shears, and edging tools can be sharpened in the same manner.

Routine Maintenance For all tools, consult the owner's manual and follow the lubricating instructions.

Your rotary lawn mower should be cleaned after each use to remove caked-on grass that has accumulated on the underside of the deck. (Remember to disconnect the spark plug wire.) Also, a simple spring and fall maintenance routine will provide longer engine life and cut down on needless repairs.

• Spring—Drain the oil by removing the drain plug on the underside of the deck. Refill with S.A.E. 30 oil formulated for two- and four-cycle engines. Remove the air filter, wash it in soapy water, dry it completely, then lightly soak it in some of the engine oil. (This procedure may have to be repeated several times during the cutting season if your cutting area is particularly dusty.) Replace the spark plug with a mower plug that has been gapped at .030. Fill the tank with fresh gasoline, and you are ready to begin cutting.

• Fall—Run the mower to empty the tank of gas to prevent condensation from forming in the gas lines or carburetor. Clean the lawn mower of any caked-on grass or other wastes, and store it in a dry area after removing the blade and sharpening it to guard against rusting.

Trees and Shrubs

Trees and shrubs planted around the home fill many needs and desires. They provide shade, protect the home or property from wind, soften the harsh and stark lines of buildings, add color, beauty, and graciousness to landscaping and, once established, require little care. Trees and shrubs are an invaluable part of your landscape design. They take many years to develop and are irreplaceable at maturity. If trees and shrubs are to fulfill these expectations, they must be selected carefully, planted properly, and cared for until they become established.

Selecting the Proper Tree or Shrub

When you plant a tree or shrub, you also plant color, shade, screening, shape, and background. Intended use and location on your property should govern your selection. Other important considerations in selecting trees and shrubs are:

Hardiness Consider the total environment of your area (seasonal climates, average rainfall, soil conditions, and contaminants). Determine which trees are reliably hardy to the environment which they must grow in. When you consider hardiness, look closely at extremes. Trees native to northern climates can easily withstand southern winters but will be scorched and killed by the heat of a southern summer. Trees planted north of their adapted range may grow well during mild or moderate winters but may be killed during a severe winter.

Form Be sure the mature form of a tree is appropriate to its intended use. Slim, upright trees will offer little shade for a patio. Broad-spreading trees may block or detract from the beauty of your home if planted in the wrong location.

Size Many homeowners have the unpleasant surprise of discovering that the attractive 5-foot evergreens they planted beside the front steps can grow 50 feet tall with a spread of 30 feet. A tree, however, should not be selected on the basis of potential size alone. Growth rate and longevity are factors that can make some larger trees acceptable choices for a relatively small lot. Some trees may grow to a height of 90 feet, but it may take them 100 or more years to attain that height. Other trees reach maturity in just a few years.

Undesirable Characteristics Most trees have characteristics that can be undesirable under certain conditions. Some trees and shrubs are more susceptible to disease and insects; some produce undesirable fruits that can be messy; some produce an abundance of seeds that sprout in lawns and flower beds; some have massive root systems that can crack concrete; and some have leaves that can clog sewers. A tree's characteristics should be compatible with location and use.

Availability When you have narrowed your choices to a few varieties, visit several nurseries to be sure your favorite selections are available in your area. Remember also that you get what you pay for.

Select only trees that will serve your landscaping purpose. For example, it is a mistake to plant a shade tree where a smaller, colorful tree would be more attractive and appropriate or to plant a tree that will grow to 100 feet in front of a small house where it will overpower the landscape rather than enhance its appearance. The following questions should be considered during your selection process:

1. Do you need a tree that will mature rapidly, or can you wait for it to reach its full height? How tall do you want the mature tree to be?
2. Will the tree be free from various fungi and harmful insects, or must you plan on a regular routine of maintenance and spraying?
3. Do you have the proper site for the tree? Will it grow in your soil and in your region of the country?
4. Will the tree fulfill your aesthetic needs in regard to color, size, and shape?

Shade Trees

Shade trees add lasting beauty to the landscape, increase the value of property, improve the environment, lessen heat and cold, screen unsightly areas, reduce noise and wind velocity, filter dust from the air, provide feed and shelter for birds and other wildlife, and make property more suitable for recreation. Shade trees give a property owner a feeling of permanence, dignity, and contentment.

Shade trees offer a multitude of bark and leaf textures, generally have full foilage, and grow to an average of 40 to 60 feet.

Some shade trees are native, but others were brought to the United States from other countries. Horticulturists have studied and recommended special types of both native and imported species for use as shade trees. Standard sources of specific information about trees that are adapted to a local area are state agricultural experiment stations, state universities, county agricultural agents, arboretums, parks, botanical gardens, arborists, and nurserymen.

Characteristics Shade trees may be divided into two main groups—deciduous and evergreen. Deciduous trees produce new leaves in spring. These leaves die and drop at the end of the growing season. The leaves of evergreen trees or conifers are usually needlelike and remain green year-round. The most popular shade coniferous trees are pine, spruce, and fir. They grow to an average height of 50-70 feet and are used in the same manner as deciduous trees. Some varieties can be trimmed into hedges.

Both deciduous and evergreen trees may be either broadleaf or needle leaf. Broadleaf trees bear leaves that have broadly expanded blades such as maples, oaks, and magnolias. Needle-leaf trees have narrow, linear, needlelike leaves. Pine, larch, and spruce are needle-leaf trees.

Some kinds of trees have no leaves but have scales that function as leaves. Scale-leaf trees have flattened, scalelike leaves that lie flat against the twigs. Arborvitae is a scale-leaf tree.

The size and form of different kinds of shade trees vary greatly at maturity, and individual trees may deviate widely from the standard.

Branching habits also differ among the many species. Some of the general branching habits of shade trees are shown in the following illustrations.

Deciduous trees generally grow faster than evergreens, but growth rate varies among all species and varieties. The rate of growth also depends on soil fertility, rainfall, and temperature. As trees age, their rate of growth usually slows. Nevertheless, pruning, fertilizing, and other maintenance practices can often rejuvenate old trees and stimulate young trees to grow more vigorously than normal.

The life of shade trees varies with species, climate, and soil. White oak, American elm, and sugar maple may live for 150 years. Red maple, weeping willow, and redbud may start to decline after 30 to 50 years. In densely populated cities and especially in some industrial areas, the useful life expectancy of many trees is much less than in suburban or rural areas. Diseases, insects, improper care, and air pollution can shorten the useful life of shade trees.

Some shade trees produce conspicuous flowers (magnolia, tulip, poplar, mimosa), but most have only inconspicuous flowers, and the flowering period usually is short. Generally, shade trees are selected for characteristics other than whether or not they are flowering.

In some cases, the production of fruit and seed by shade trees can be objectionable. Fruit and seed production in some species can be prevented by planting trees that produce only male flowers. Male cultivars of ginkgo, honey locust, and mulberry are available.

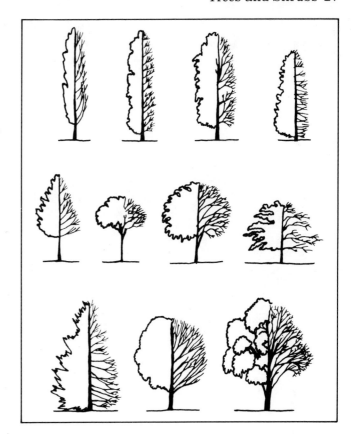

Common branching habits and tree shapes.

Selecting Shade Trees Shade trees are an enduring feature around the home, so they should be carefully selected. Cold hardiness is the primary requirement in selecting trees. Trees native to a locality can be relied on for cold hardiness, but some introduced species also can withstand winter cold. The coldest area (plant hardiness zone) in which each species will normally succeed is given in the charts.

Some species are intolerant of high temperatures. Heat and drought resistance usually are linked. If trees are watered, however, some species can be grown in hot, dry climates where they would not otherwise survive. Nevertheless, in areas of low rainfall, drought resistant species require less care than trees that must be watered.

Some species grow poorly or die if the soil in which they are planted is too alkaline or too acid. Soils may be too wet or too dry for some species to grow well or even survive.

The rate of growth of different kinds of shade trees is another factor to consider. In general, trees that grow rapidly have weak wood that is easily damaged by storms and decay. Trees that grow more slowly have stronger wood, making them more durable. However, if quick shade is needed, the use of fast-growing trees may be justified.

The size and shape of trees at maturity also

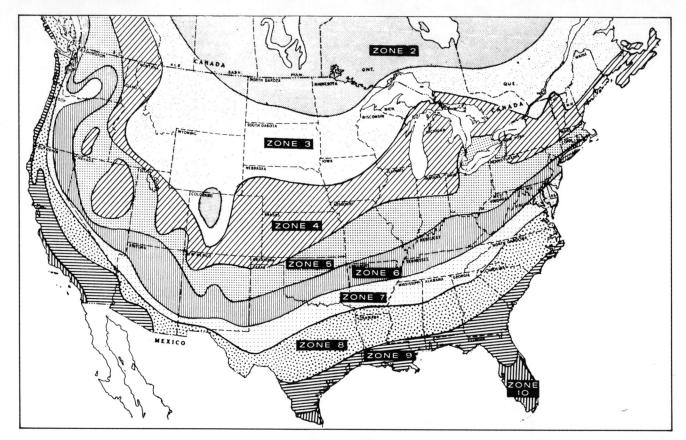

should be considered. A tree 35 feet tall at maturity is acceptable on the average city lot with a one-story house. Trees 50 to 100 feet high would be too tall for such a lot but would be suitable for large yards.

Examine the locations where you plan to plant shade trees carefully. Certain trees may have characteristics that may cause problems. Roots of elms, willows, poplars, and maples, for example, can clog sewers. These trees should not be planted near drainage pipes.

The roots of some trees grow near the surface of the soil. If they are planted near a sidewalk, roots may break the pavement. Also, tree roots near the surface rob grass of water and can interfere with lawn mowing. Avoid planting shade trees beneath telephone and power lines. Trees that grow over the roof of a house can fill the gutters with leaves, but these trees also shade the house from the hot summer sun.

The kind of shade that is desired can be provided where and when it is needed by careful selection of the species and the planting site. Norway maple gives dense shade, but honey locust gives light, dappled shade. Evergreens keep their color and give shade throughout the year, but deciduous trees do not. The brilliant autumn foliage of some species may influence the choice if other characteristics are equal.

Some species are so easily damaged by diseases or insects that control measures are essential. The

Hardiness Zone Map. Refer to the above map when using the charts throughout this book which include a reference to the hardiness zone. Average minimum temperatures for each zone are: (1) northern Canada, (2) -50° to -35°, (3) -35° to -20°, (4) -20° to -10°, (5) -10° to -5°, (6) -5° to 5°, (7) 5° to 10°, (8) 10° to 20°, (9) 20° to 30°, and (10) 30° to 40°.

American elm is seriously threatened by Dutch elm disease. Box elder is frequently a host of box-elder bugs, which have an obnoxious odor and often overwinter in houses.

Some trees, such as horse chestnut, produce hard, poisonous fruits that are dangerous if eaten. Fruits can be a nuisance in lawns, stain concrete surfaces, or smell bad when decaying.

Trees such as Siberian elm, poplar, red maple, and mimosa produce abundant crops of seeds that become a nuisance in lawns and gardens. Some trees such as the honey locust sprout from the roots, and the sprouts often interfere with lawn mowing. Although flowers of most trees are attractive and last only a short time, they can cause discomfort to persons allergic to their pollen.

It is difficult to find a species that has no faults. The faults of trees must be balanced against the good qualities in deciding what kind to plant. Select the shade trees that best serve your landscape design, purpose, and needs. The following charts list popular deciduous and coniferous trees and their average heights, growth rates, and primary characteristics, and the regions where they grow best.

BROADLEAF DECIDUOUS SHADE TREES

Tree	Height Feet	Growth Rate	Primary Characteristics	1	2	3	4	5	6	7	8	9	10
Norway Maple	35-55	Mod. to fast	Grows in wide range of soils, casts heavy shade	X	X			X	X	X	X	X	
Sycamore Maple	35-75	Mod. to fast	Very long life-span, requires space, salt tolerant		X	X	X	X	X				
Red Maple	40-80	Mod. to fast	Long life-span, brilliant autumn foliage	X	X	X		X			X	X	
Sugar Maple	45-75	Mod. to fast	Brilliant autumn foliage, popular shade tree	X			X	X	X	X		X	
Silver Maple	35-55	Fast	Grows in wide range of soils, weak wood		X	X	X		X				
White Oak	60-100	Slow	Very long life-span, one of the best shade trees					X	X	X	X	X	X
English Oak	50-90	Slow to mod.	Very long life-span, grows in wide range of soils					X	X	X		X	
Scarlet Oak	60-80	Mod. to fast	Long life-span, brilliant autumn foliage				X	X	X	X			
Pin Oak	50-85	Fast	Grows in wide range of soils, easy transplant			X	X	X	X	X			
Holly Oak	35-55	Mod. to fast	Grows best in coastal areas and inland valleys							X	X	X	X
Black Oak	60-90	Mod.	Deep-rooted tree, grows in wide range of soils	X	X	X	X			X			
Willow Oak	55-90	Mod. to fast	Long life-span, excellent shade tree					X	X	X		X	
Chestnut Oak	60-90	Mod. to fast	Grows well under harsh, rocky soil conditions	X		X	X		X				
Northern Red Oak	60-85	Mod.	Tolerates city conditions well, bright foliage	X		X					X	X	
Black Ash	30-40	Mod. to fast	Grows best in moist soils, average life-span					X		X	X		
White Ash	40-75	Fast	Long life-span, requires large amounts of water					X	X	X	X	X	X
Modesto Ash	30-40	Mod. to fast	Grows in many soils, good shade tree					X		X	X	X	X
Green Ash	40-60	Mod. to fast	Seeds can be a nuisance in gardens	X				X	X	X		X	
White Birch	25-50	Fast	Beautiful white bark, requires drought protection	X	X	X	X	X				X	
Paper Birch	35-70	Fast	Peeling white bark, requires drought protection	X	X	X	X	X	X				
American Beech	60-85	Mod.	Long life-span, grows in many soils, surface roots					X	X	X	X	X	
European Beech	45-85	Mod.	Beautifully shaped tree, adaptable to many soils		X			X	X	X	X		
American Elm	50-75	Mod. to fast	Susceptible to disease, a favorite shade tree					X	X	X	X	X	
Chinese Elm	50-65	Fast	Disease tolerant, grows in wide range of soils					X	X	X	X	X	
Scotch Elm	65-80	Mod. to fast	Somewhat disease tolerant, susceptible to insects				X		X	X	X		
Honey Locust	35-70	Fast	Adaptable to many soils, casts light shade	X	X	X	X	X	X	X	X	X	X
Black Locust	40-70	Fast	Long life-span, grows in many soils, flowers in spring	X		X	X	X	X	X	X	X	X
Horse Chestnut	30-55	Mod.	Grows best on well-drained soil, flowers in spring		X	X	X	X	X		X		
Walnut	50-80	Mod. to fast	Produces edible nuts, attractive autumn foliage		X	X	X	X	X	X			
Bitternut Hickory	50-70	Mod. to fast	Grows on wide range of soils, produces nuts					X	X	X	X	X	X
Shagbark Hickory	70-95	Slow	Long life-span, grows on wide range of soils					X	X	X	X	X	X
Pecan	50-90	Fast	Long life-span, produces edible nuts			X	X	X	X	X			
Apple	25-50	Mod. to fast	Flowers in spring, bears edible fruit	X	X	X	X	X	X				
Aspen	50-75	Fast	Weak wood, not heat tolerant	X	X	X							
Catalpa	40-70	Fast	Grows in wide variety of soils, hardy	X	X	X		X	X	X			
Cottonwood	50-90	Fast	Males do not produce "cotton" substance					X	X	X	X		
Ginkgo	60-95	Mod. to fast	Long life-span, highly resistant to disease					X	X	X	X		
Hackberry	55-80	Mod.	Grows well in hot, dry areas					X	X	X	X	X	X
Hornbeam	25-50	Slow	Grows in wide range of soils, brilliant foliage					X	X	X	X	X	X
American Linden	50-70	Mod. to fast	Fragrant summer flowers, city tolerant				X	X	X	X	X	X	X
Little-leaf Linden	35-50	Mod.	Very city tolerant, grows in many soils				X	X	X	X	X	X	
London Plane	50-70	Fast	Pollution resistant, grows in many soils						X	X	X	X	
Magnolia	40-80	Mod.	Large beautiful flowers, long life-span								X	X	X
Mimosa	25-40	Fast	Not hardy, summer flowers								X	X	X
Mulberry	50-90	Mod.	Very long life-span, city tolerant				X	X	X	X		X	
Poplar	35-60	Fast	Susceptible to some diseases				X		X	X	X		
Redbud	25-35	Mod. to fast	Relatively short life-span			X	X	X	X				
Serviceberry	25-40	Mod. to fast	Attractive flowers and fruit			X	X	X	X				
Sweetgum	60-90	Mod.	Bright autumn foliage, moist, well-drained soil						X	X	X	X	
Sycamore	75-100	Fast	Long life-span, sheds bark			X	X	X					
Tulip Poplar	45-80	Fast	Very long life-span, surface roots					X	X	X			
Willow	25-40	Fast	Requires moist soil, sheds twigs and branches					X	X	X	X	X	X
Zelkova	50-75	Fast	Related to elm tree, disease resistant					X	X	X	X	X	X

Norway Maple	White Oak	White Ash	White Birch	American Beech
American Elm	Honey Locust	Horse Chestnut	Shagbark Hickory	Black Walnut
Quaking Aspen	Weeping Willow	American Basswood (Linden)	Poplar (Cottonwood)	American Sycamore
White Pine	Red Pine	Giant Arborvitae	Cedar of Lebanon	Red Cedar
Western (Canada) Hemlock	Blue Spruce	(Hollywood) Juniper	White Fir	Upright Japanese Yew

Favorite American deciduous trees can be found in the first three rows. The last two rows include popular evergreen trees.

CONIFEROUS AND BROADLEAF EVERGREEN TREES

Tree	Height Feet	Growth Rate	Primary Characteristics	1	2	3	4	5	6	7	8	9	10
Austrian Pine	30-50	Mod. to fast	Does not tolerate severe winter conditions						X	X	X	X	X
Eastern White Pine	35-90	Mod.	Tall graceful shape			X	X	X	X	X			
Ponderosa Pine	40-75	Mod.	Long life-span, adapts well to many soils			X	X	X	X	X			
American Red Pine	30-60	Mod. to fast	Somewhat susceptible to insects	X	X	X	X	X					
Scotch Pine	25-50	Mod.	Long life-span, grows best on sandy loam		X	X	X	X	X				
American Arborvitae	15-50	Slow to Mod.	Long life-span, requires well-drained soil			X	X		X	X	X	X	
Giant Arborvitae	60-90	Mod. to fast	Requires well-drained soil, moderate life-span				X	X	X	X	X	X	X
Oriental Arborvitae	25-40	Slow	Available in several sizes and shapes						X	X	X	X	
Japanese Arborvitae	25-40	Slow	Requires well-drained soil, spreading						X	X	X		
Eastern Red Cedar	35-75	Mod.	Grows best in well-drained soils	X	X	X	X	X	X	X			
Cedar of Lebanon	50-100	Mod.	Very long life-span, ideally suited to Southeast						X	X	X	X	
Incense Cedar	60-90	Mod.	Long life-span, not susceptible to insects						X	X	X	X	X
Silver Red Cedar	30-60	Mod.	Very stately pine shape					X	X	X	X	X	
Atlas Cedar	50-90	Mod. to fast	Grows best on well-drained soils							X	X	X	X
Deodara Cedar	50-85	Mod.	Branches form close to the ground								X	X	X
White Fir	60-90	Mod. to fast	Tolerates heat, drought and poor soil conditions			X	X	X	X	X	X		
Douglas Fir	50-80	Slow	Requires moist, but well-drained soil				X	X	X	X	X		
Canadian Hemlock	60-90	Slow to mod.	Requires moist, but well-drained soil		X	X	X	X	X	X	X		
Carolina Hemlock	50-70	Mod. to fast	Requires partial shade, can be trimmed as hedge		X	X	X	X	X				
Western Hemlock	40-75	Mod.	Requires moist, but well-drained soil					X	X	X	X		
Colorado Blue Spruce	75-100	Slow	Grows best on sandy loam, use as accent		X	X	X	X	X	X			
Red Spruce	55-70	Slow	Long life-span, grows best on well-drained soil		X	X	X	X	X				
White Spruce	35-40	Slow	Tolerates slightly acid soil			X	X	X	X				
Norway Spruce	60-100	Slow	Large stately conifer, needs well-drained soil		X	X	X	X		X			
Rocky Mountain Juniper	20-30	Mod.	Long life-span, grows on wide range of soils			X	X	X	X	X	X		
Chinese Juniper	15-30	Mod.	Winter injury can be severe					X	X	X	X	X	
American Holly	15-45	Slow	Requires moist, but well-drained soil					X	X	X	X	X	
Chinese Holly	15-35	Slow	Moderate life-span, moist but well-drained soil						X	X	X	X	X
English Holly	15-50	Slow	Many cultivars available								X	X	
Japanese Holly	10-12	Slow	Foliage similar to boxwood tree					X	X	X		X	
Japanese Yew	15-30	Slow	A very dense, pyramidal small evergreen		X	X	X	X	X				
Intermediate Yew	15-25	Slow	Narrow and conical in form		X	X	X	X	X				
California Laurel	40-75	Mod.	Long life-span, grows best in coastal areas								X	X	X
Laurel Cherry	35-60	Mod.	Attractive flowers, needs fertile soil								X	X	X
Grecian Laurel	12-40	Slow	Aromatic foliage, moist sandy soil							X	X	X	X
Indian Laurel Fig	25-50	Mod.	Adaptable to many soils, surface roots								X	X	X
Moreton Bay Fig	50-75	Fast	Long life-span, casts heavy shade							X	X	X	X
Fiddle-Leaf Fig	40-60	Mod.	Requires moist soil									X	X
Russian Olive	15-30	Fast	Grows in wide range of soils and climates	X	X	X	X	X	X	X	X	X	X
Camphor Tree	30-75	Slow	Grows best in warm coastal and valley areas								X	X	X
Carob	30-50	Mod.	Dense shade, heat tolerant								X	X	X

Planting Shade Trees

Shade trees may be obtained with the soil held around their roots by burlap, wire, or plastic. They are known as balled and burlapped trees. Trees that come in containers are commonly known as container grown trees, and those sold without soil on the roots are called bare-rooted trees. Balled and burlapped and container-grown trees generally have a higher rate of survival. Balled and burlapped trees should have a root ball measuring 1 foot in diameter for each inch of the tree trunk diameter.

Nursery-grown trees usually have a better chance of survival than trees dug from the woods because root systems of nursery-grown trees usually are compact and less likely to be injured seriously when they are dug. Many arborists, nurserymen, and landscape contractors guarantee trees planted by them for at least one year.

Many kinds of wild trees can be transplanted satisfactorily if the roots are carefully preserved. If wild trees are moved, the roots should be pruned approximately one year before they are dug. New roots then have time to develop around the perimeter of the pruned roots. A more compact root system is formed, and most of it can be dug without damage. Small wild trees usually withstand transplanting better than large ones.

Trees of almost any size can be transplanted successfully if proper equipment is available. Trees with a trunk diameter of 1.5 to 3 inches may be planted with bare roots, but larger trees should be balled and burlapped and transplanted without disturbing the roots any more than necessary. Generally, as trees get larger, they cost more to buy and transplant. A professional should be obtained to move large trees.

Planting Seasons The most favorable planting season for shade trees varies with the region, kind of tree, soil, source of planting stock, and method of handling. The method of handling is the way that trees are grown, dug, stored, and transported.

In general, deciduous trees are planted in autumn after their leaves change color and before the ground freezes; or they are planted in late winter or early spring after the ground has thawed, but before buds start to grow. However, spring is considered the best time to plant in areas where the ground freezes deeply, where strong winds prevail, or where soil moisture is deficient. The drying effects of strong winds can be reduced by watering the trees and wrapping the trunk and larger limbs with burlap or special protective paper. Spring is the best time to plant bare-rooted trees.

In the upper South, balled and burlapped or container-grown deciduous trees may be planted in winter whenever the ground is not frozen. In the deep South, in warmer parts of California, and in southwest Texas, small bare-rooted deciduous trees also may be planted during winter. In the coastal areas of northern California, the best time to plant is autumn before freezing weather.

In cold regions, needle-leaf evergreens such as pine, spruce, juniper, and arborvitae usually are planted early in the fall or in spring after the ground has thawed. Needle-leaf evergreens that are balled and burlapped or canned may be planted in cold regions anytime the ground is workable. They should be mulched and watered after planting.

In warm regions, needle-leaf evergreens may be planted anytime if the trees are watered regularly. Small needle-leaf evergreens may be planted bare rooted. The chances for large ones to survive are better if they are balled and burlapped.

Spring is the best season to plant such broad-leaved evergreens as magnolia and holly, but they may be planted in autumn if time is allowed for the roots to grow before the ground freezes.

The best time to plant palms is during warm, wet months, but they may be planted anytime if they are adequately watered after planting.

Temporary Storage Trees should be planted as soon as possible after they are dug or purchased from a nursery. If they must be held for several days, the roots must be kept moist in a cool area. Roots die if allowed to dry out. When watering be careful not to wash away any of the soil in the ball.

The roots of balled and burlapped trees should be sprinkled as needed to keep the soil from drying, and the tops should be sprinkled on windy or hot days. Also, the tops and roots of balled and burlapped trees may be covered with plastic or canvas, or with plastic over wet burlap. In any case, do not allow the roots to dry.

Bare-rooted trees that cannot be planted immediately after they are delivered may be heeled-in. To heel-in a tree, dig a trench with one sloping side. Spread the roots in the trench with the trunk resting against the sloping side. Then cover the roots with soil or a loose, moist mulch of straw, peat moss, or similar organic material. Keep the mulch moist until the trees are planted. Protect the tops of heeled-in trees as much as possible from drying winds. Locate the heeling-in bed in a shady place if possible.

Spacing Plant shade trees as far apart as their mature limb spread is expected to be so they can develop to their full mature size without crowding each other. Most shade trees should be planted at least 30 feet from a house. On narrow streets and in congested areas, use trees that are relatively small at maturity.

A few suggested spacing distances between trees are: American elm, 60 feet; white pine, 45 feet; oaks such as willow, red, pin, scarlet, white, black, or water, 60 feet; live oak, 80 to 100 feet; littleleaf linden, 40 feet; southern magnolia, 40 feet; spruce, 40 feet; and sugar or red maple, 50 feet.

Preparing the Planting Hole Dig the planting hole for bare-rooted trees wide enough so the roots can be spread in their natural position. Roots should not be doubled back. The planting hole for a balled and burlapped or canned tree should be about 2 feet wider than the diameter of the root ball or container so that fertile soil can be put around the roots.

The hole should be deep enough for the tree to be planted as deep as it was originally. However, if the soil is poorly drained, the hole should be 4 inches or more deeper so a drainage system can be installed.

Planting holes must be well drained for most trees to grow satisfactorily. Most species will not grow well, and some will not survive if they are planted where water stands for even a short time. Drainage can be provided by putting one or two lines of 3- or 4-inch tile and a layer of gravel or crushed rock in the bottom of the hole. For holes 5 to 6 feet across, one line of tile usually is sufficient. For holes more than 6 feet across, at least two lines of tile are recommended. The bottom of the planting hole should be sloped so that excess water will run to the side. The tile then should be placed across the bottom of the hole and extended beyond the hole to a free outlet. The outlet may drain into a ground level lower than the bottom of the hole, a dry well filled with gravel, or a storm sewer. Never connect the tile to a sanitary sewer because the roots can grow into sanitary sewers and clog them.

After the tile is laid, carefully spread enough

gravel or crushed rock over the bottom of the hole to hold the tile in place and cover it. Put glass cloth or roofing paper over the tile to help keep soil out of the drainage system. Then spread 2 to 3 inches of fertile soil over the bottom.

If the ground has a hardpan underlaid with permeable soil, the planting site can sometimes be drained by punching holes through the hardpan and filling the holes with gravel or crushed rock. In the dry Southwest, it may be necessary to dig holes several feet deep to penetrate the hardpan and get good drainage. Often the best solution to poor drainage is to select a tree that will tolerate it.

If the soil is very low in fertility, mix fertilizer with the soil. Well-decayed leaf mold, steamed bonemeal, or similar organic material may be used. For trees 6 to 10 feet tall, mix about one-half pound of 5-10-5, 4-12-4, or a similar complete fertilizer with each 4 bushels of filling soil. The fertilizer will help stimulate early growth. Too much fertilizer will burn the roots.

Soil acidity is generally expressed as a pH value. A pH of 7.0 is neutral, below 7.0 is acid, and above 7.0 is alkaline. Adding lime decreases acidity, and adding sulphur or aluminum sulfate increases acidity. A pH of 6.0 to 7.0 is suitable for most shade trees. Generally, most needle-leaf evergreens grow best in acid soil, but junipers will grow in nearly neutral soil.

Usually, county agricultural agents, state agricultural experiment stations, or state agricultural colleges will test soil to determine acidity and the need for fertilizer. Some states charge a fee for the service.

Steps for Planting Trees and Shrubs:
1. Dig a generous hole one-half again as large as the root ball, making sure that the walls are perpendicular and the bottom of the hole is flat. This will ensure proper root development and growth.
2. Mix thoroughly one-half the recommended quantity of peat and manure with your best soil, and place the mixture in the bottom of the hole, forming a slight mound for the root ball to rest on.
3. Trim off any exposed roots that are broken or damaged. Prune the plant about one-third from the top. Remove all branches but make sure that you preserve the tree's original form.
4. Remove the packing from the root ball unless it is burlap, which will decompose. Place the plant on the mound so that it stands straight and faces the direction you want. The top of the root ball should be about 1 inch below grade.
5. Mix the remaining peat moss and manure with good soil taken from the hole. Backfill with this mixture, covering two-thirds of the root ball. Then firm the soil, and water.

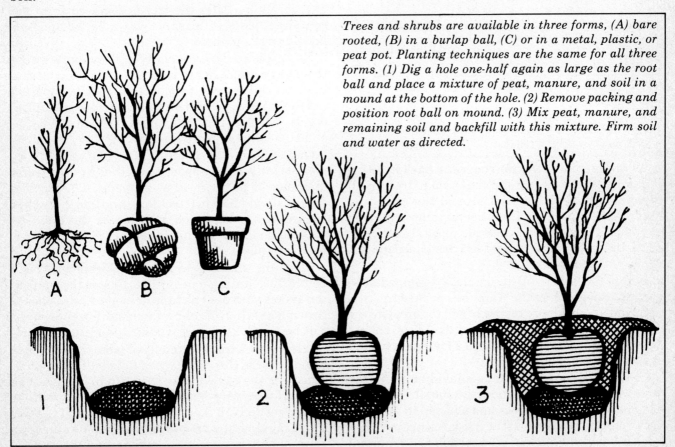

Trees and shrubs are available in three forms, (A) bare rooted, (B) in a burlap ball, (C) or in a metal, plastic, or peat pot. Planting techniques are the same for all three forms. (1) Dig a hole one-half again as large as the root ball and place a mixture of peat, manure, and soil in a mound at the bottom of the hole. (2) Remove packing and position root ball on mound. (3) Mix peat, manure, and remaining soil and backfill with this mixture. Firm soil and water as directed.

6. After the water has drained away, finish back-filling the hole. Leave a 1-inch trough around the circle to collect water.
7. Discard all gravel, stone, or clay.
8. Water twice weekly for the first month until the plant becomes well established.

Setting the Tree If possible, trees with trunks 6 inches or more in diameter should be set with the trunk facing the same direction it was facing in its original site. Smaller trees may be set without regard to orientation.

When trees with bare roots are set in the hole, they should be held in place while the roots are adjusted to their natural position and covered with soil. If fertile loam was removed from the hole, it may be used to cover the roots. Loam is usually sufficiently permeable to air and water for good growth of shade trees.

Heavy clay soil has poor permeability. It can be made more permeable by mixing it with as much sand as necessary to obtain good percolation of water. Sandy soil may be made less permeable by mixing it with loam, clay, and organic material such as peat moss. Do not use fresh manure or fresh green plant material in the planting hole because these materials release compounds when they decay that are toxic to tree roots. Often the best solution is to use well-composted soil or topsoil for covering the roots.

TREATMENT OF SOIL BEFORE PLANTING TREES AND SHRUBS

Plant Size	Humus	Composted Manure
15-18 inches	12 lbs.	8 lbs.
18-24 inches	23 lbs.	12 lbs.
2- 5 feet	33 lbs.	15 lbs.
5-10 feet	50 lbs.	25 lbs.
10-15 feet	100 lbs.	50 lbs.

Work the soil among the roots and pack it with a blunt tool. Gently sway and shake small trees in all directions to settle the soil around the roots and eliminate air pockets. Continue to tamp and pack the soil as it is added. When the roots are covered, tamp the soil so that it is settled firmly around the roots. Do not tamp wet soil.

Before the hole is filled completely, add water to settle the soil. When the water has soaked into the soil, add about 2 more inches of soil to complete the backfill. Do not pack this soil. A ridge of soil should be added around the rim to form a low basin to hold water over the root area.

Balled and burlapped trees should be set in the hole with the burlap around the root ball. If the hole is too deep, lift small trees and add soil to raise the ball to the proper level. If the tree is too heavy to lift, rock it back and forth in all directions and ram soil

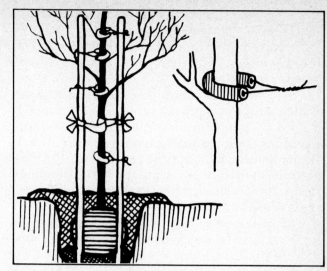

This is the proper method of supporting a tree with stakes to ensure straight, healthy growth.

beneath the ball until it is at the proper height. Loosen the burlap and drop it from the side of the ball. The burlap does not need to be entirely removed from beneath the ball.

A hard crust sometimes forms on the surface of the ball. Break the crust before filling the planting hole. Pack the filling soil as it is added. Settle it with water the same as for bare-rooted trees.

If the tree is in a container, cut away the sides of the container with metal shears and remove the root ball carefully. After the tree is removed from the container, plant it the same way a balled and burlapped tree is planted.

Newly planted trees usually need support to hold them in position and to keep the roots from loosening and the crowns from breaking. Unsupported trees often lean permanently away from prevailing winds. At planting, bracing stakes should be installed before the roots are covered.

One to three wooden stakes or one metal fence post usually will support trees that have a trunk diameter of no more than 2 inches. The wooden stakes should be 6 to 9 feet long and 2 to 2½ inches square at the base and bevelled at the top. The stakes should be strong enough to hold the trunk rigidly in place.

Place the stakes 3 to 18 inches from the trunk before the planting hole is filled. Fasten the trunk to the stakes with canvas tape or loops of wire passed through a section of rubber or plastic hose or similar soft material. Bare wire will scrape or cut the bark.

A tree with a trunk diameter of more than 2 inches usually needs three guy wires to hold it securely in place. Fix the guy wires so they can be tightened as needed. One wire should be fastened to a stake driven securely in the ground on the side of the tree that is against the prevailing winds. The other two wires should be spaced equally around the tree.

The stakes should slope away from the tree at approximately a right angle to the slope of the guy wires. A heavy log or beam (deadman) may be used instead of a stake to anchor the guy wires. Fasten the guy wires about two-thirds of the way up the trunk of the tree.

Stakes and wires are usually removed as soon as the tree roots are firmly established in the ground, usually after one year. A small tree planted with a ball of earth around the roots may not need guy wires.

Caring for Shade Trees After Planting

Trees should be watered as needed during the first and second growing seasons after they are planted. Watering thoroughly once a week is better than light daily watering. Do not saturate the soil so much that water can be squeezed from it by hand. Sandy soil requires more water than does clay soil. Trees may be deep watered with a special needle or through previously installed pipe or gravel-filled openings.

Frequent light misting of the tops of newly planted evergreens in early morning or late afternoon will help the leaves. Evergreens planted in autumn should be watered frequently to provide them with plenty of soil moisture before the ground freezes.

To protect the trunk of a newly planted deciduous tree from pests and from dying, wrap it spirally with strips of burlap or specially prepared crepe paper. Strips of kraft paper may be used, but special crepe paper is easier to handle. Some wraps are also treated to increase protection against trunk-boring insects. Overlap each turn one-half the width of the strip. Reinforce the wrapping with stout cord wrapped spirally in the direction opposite to that of the paper. Tie the cord at intervals as necessary to hold the paper in place. Leave the wrap on the trunk for two years. If it rots away sooner, replace it. Trunks of evergreens seldom need wrapping.

When trees are planted in the fall, mulch them when they are planted. When trees are planted in the spring, mulch them after the soil has warmed. Place the mulch over the entire root area to help hold moisture in the soil and stabilize the temperature. Leave the mulch around the trees until it decays. Two to 3 inches of peat moss, leaf mold, pine needles, oat or peanut hulls, ground corncobs, straw, or similar material may be used. Fiberglass or jute mesh are good materials for mulching trees on slopes. Broad-leaved evergreens should be mulched continuously. In humid areas, mulching may not be needed.

Pruning The purposes of pruning are to control the size and shape of your plants, and to remove damaged, diseased, or old wood that will retard growth. Proper pruning will improve and maintain your tree's health and appearance.

You can prune a deciduous tree to keep its natural size and shape by thinning overcrowded branches and by cutting back for proper direction of new growth. New growth will follow the direction that the existing buds are pointing. So before you prune, try to visualize which way the new growth will head after it appears. When pruning dead wood or diseased branches, cut about 1 inch below the damaged area into live, healthy wood.

If it is necessary to eliminate an entire branch, cut it off flush with the stem or trunk. If it is larger than 1 inch in diameter, apply a tree paint to protect against disease or fungus.

To control the size of the plant, thin or cut out stray branches or stems. Branches are usually cut back to a larger branch, and the needless stems can be cut off at ground level. This thinning not only enables air to circulate through the tree but allows room for the growth of side branches that make the tree or shrub fuller and bushier. When first thinning, cut out only the older, taller stems. Prune each limb individually and purposefully. Try to preserve the inherent branching characteristics of the tree. Do not attempt a major pruning job all at once. Cut only about one-quarter of the tree each year, or the tree will have little foliage and give a bare appearance to your landscape.

Trees planted with bare roots usually have some roots missing. To compensate for the loss of roots, prune out about one-third of the top. Pruning is not necessary in humid areas. New roots usually will grow within a few weeks and restore normal water absorption. Balled and burlapped and container-grown trees usually need no pruning when planted.

After trees are established, they should be pruned to shape them or to remove dead, diseased, or severely damaged parts. Reduce top growth by pruning whole branches, if possible, unless the tree has few branches and would be mutilated if whole branches were removed. Cut close to the trunk or a branch fork and do not leave short stubs. Do not prune the central leader of trees that normally have only one, such as pin oak, pine, or spruce. If the central leader of these trees is removed, they will be disfigured and a new leader will not grow for many years.

Diseases, insects, animals, and lawn mowers or other tools may damage newly planted trees. Use an antiseptic tree wound paint on wounds 1½ inches or more in diameter. County agricultural agents and state agricultural experiment stations can provide information on the control of diseases and insects.

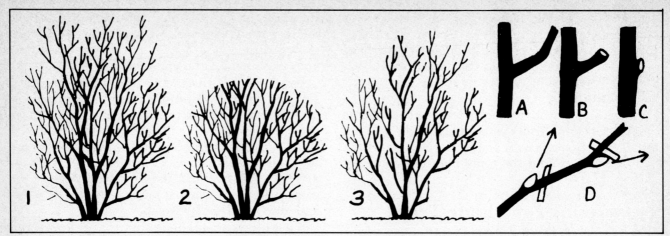

(1) A shrub requiring pruning. (2) Incorrect pruning method. (3) Correct pruning method. (A) A branch needing pruning. (B) Incorrect pruning method. (C) Correct pruning method. (D) The direction of growth can be controlled by pruning just above buds.

The wrapping on trunks may give some protection against rodents and dogs. Stakes and guy wires help reduce damage by lawn mowers and other small mechanical devices. Sometimes a fence may be necessary to protect a small tree.

Pruning Tools The three tools most needed for pruning are hand pruning shears, lopping shears, and a sharp pruning saw. The hand shears are used to cut the smaller branches and twigs. The cut must be even through the wood to allow for quick healing. Use lopping shears to cut branches that are up to 1½ inches in diameter and are difficult to reach with a saw. For branches over 1½ inches, use a pruning saw. It should have coarse teeth set far apart for a quick and even cut with little damage to the tree. If you saw off branches over 1½ inches in diameter, you should apply tree paint to guard against disease and fungus infection.

When to Prune

- Deciduous, Nonflowering Trees and Shrubs—Prune all deciduous, nonflowering trees in the early fall, just after the leaves have dropped. At this time you will be able to see the branch structure and better determine what to eliminate.
- Spring-Flowering Trees and Shrubs—The blossoms of spring-flowering trees and shrubs are formed on the growth produced the previous year. If you prune them in the fall or winter months, you will destroy many or all of the buds that would produce blossoms in the spring. Prune these plants after their spring flowers have faded. The more common spring-flowering trees and shrubs are azalea, beautybush, crab, dogwood, firethorn, forsythia, honeysuckle, hydrangea, lilac, magnolia, mock orange, and spirea.
- Summer-Flowering Trees and Shrubs—Plants that flower during the summer produce their buds from wood grown that season. It is advisable to prune these plants in the early spring just before any growth would begin. Some of

the plants that fit into this grouping are abelia, bush clover, elder (red berry), heather, honeysuckle bush, sumac, and summersweet.

- Coniferous Evergreens—Prune evergreens so that each type will develop an individual shape and become compact rather than straggly. It is best to prune them in May or June, after the new shoots have formed. With annual maintenance, you will have to prune only the new growth. Prune the many thick branches with small hand pruners to give them a natural look. Pruning with electric hedge clippers is quicker and easier, but unless care is taken the plant will have an artificial, harsh appearance. Plants that belong to the coniferous evergreen family include arborvitae, fir, hemlock, juniper, pine, spruce, and yew.
- Broad-leaved Evergreens—Broad-leaved evergreens, such as the andromeda, camellia, holly, leucothoe, mountain laurel, and rhododendron, should be pruned immediately after they have flowered. When pruning to promote new growth, cut back to the bud or to a newly formed shoot; otherwise you may cut too far and eliminate new growth for the next growing season.
- Hedges—Take out any dead wood in the early spring. Prune when there is approximately 3 to 6 inches of new growth, and remove only half the new growth each time until the desired height is reached. Thereafter you can prune as often as desired. It is important to cut the top of the hedge slightly narrower than the bottom so that the lower parts of the plants will receive sunlight and water.

Fertilizing Shade trees that do well are often taken for granted. However, they will yield better growth if they are fertilized once a year, even though

Flowering shrubs and trees are very popular landscaping elements, and among the favorites are the flowering crab apple (above), apple tree (blossoms immediately below), lilac (lower left), and hydrangea (lower center). All photos courtesy of Jerry Koser

Flowering shrubs can be arranged to provide depth, texture, and beautiful color to the landscape plan. This background arrangement offers a wide variety of colors in spring and summer with flowers and in fall with bright foliage.

The garden flowers on this page beginning with the top row, from left to right, are: snapdragons, Turk's-cap lily, yellow iris, primrose, daffodils, lily-of-the-valley, painted daisies, rudbeckia, and delphinium.

Flower beds (upper left corner and above) are the best way to showcase your garden flowers. Plan to arrange flowers according to their height, color, and time of blossom for the most stunning and beautiful design.

The garden flowers on this page, beginning with the photo at right, are: impatiens, pansies and marigolds, blue asters, petunias, salmon-colored rose, and yellow roses. All photos on these two pages courtesy of Jerry Koser

When arranging flower beds, select complementary colors, such as the shades of blue, above, for a soft, cool appearance, or contrasting shades of colors, as in the tulip bed, below, for a lively, bright appearance.

The foundation planting of this landscape design (left) focuses attention to the large window area of the family-room addition. Note how the red foliage contrasts beautifully with the evergreen shrubs.

The clean, crisp lines of the hedge along the foundation help to balance the informal areas of ground cover adjacent to the front walk in this design (above right). The strong vertical lines of the trees also help to balance the strong horizontal lines of the hedge.

The vertical lines of this colonial home (lower right) are balanced by the symmetrical horizontal lines of the foundation planting. One corner of the home is partially hidden by a low-growing fringe tree. The yellow forsythia and the evergreen shrubs add color contrast.

This recently landscaped property (left) utilizes plants around the walk area that are interesting in all seasons: for winter, evergreens; for spring and summer, flowering shrubs; and for fall, brilliant foliage. When the shrubs mature, they will prevent car-lights from shining through the windows.

Ivy and evergreen shrubs have turned this home-site (below) into a green, lush area. A few flowers at the base of the shrubs and the flower box provide enough color contrast to create an attractive total effect.

A low fieldstone wall, enhanced by low-growing perennial flowers (right), provides a natural frame for the entire property. A wooden footbridge spans a small ravine in the background.

Approach plantings are an essential part of every landscape. They invite and draw visitors to the home's entrance. Shrubs and trees lead a visitor to the front entrance of the home (above left). A walk leads from the garage/drive area to the patio entrance (lower left). A windscreen of upright evergreen shrubs provides privacy and protection for the patio area.

The landscape around this beautiful stone patio is relatively open to provide an unobstructed view of the pond at the back of the property.

Large trees and wide-spreading shrubs provide privacy for this split-level home (above). The entrance to the drive is accented with a variety of evergreen shrubs adding year-round interest.

Slopes require special treatment. Lawn areas can be utilized on slopes provided the grade is gradual (above left). To allow for easy maintenance on hard-to-mow slopes (lower left), the area is best planted with ground covers or flowers.

The driveway of this home (below) is several feet below the entrance to the home. The area between was terraced to provide beauty and balance to the landscape.

Because evergreens offer a wide variety of colors, shapes, and textures and generally keep their foliage year-round, they are popular choices for many landscape uses.

The entrance to this property (above) features a post and rail fence surrounded by shrubs to provide color and texture throughout the year. This area attractively calls attention to the drive.

The driveway is an important landscape area. It is generally the first impression people receive and should, therefore, set the tone for your design. Short drives (above left) need a screen to conceal car headlights. Long drives (lower left) can be a beautiful tunnel of living color while secluding the house from view.

A light near the drive entrance (below) welcomes visitors and serves as an excellent vertical focal point in a horizontal shrub planting.

This design, similar to the one above, uses a fieldstone corner to indicate the property's border.

Berms (a slightly raised mound) are very popular elements in contemporary landscape design. Trees and shrubs can be surrounded with mulch for neat appearance and easy maintenance.

Rock gardens are a beautiful, natural background. Taller shrubs behind the rock garden block the view of surrounding buildings while providing a colorful background for the overall design.

their roots are deep and broad. Spring feeding is generally recommended to stimulate healthier, richer-looking growth. Apply fertilizer when the buds begin to swell. An acceptable time to fertilize is fall, after the leaves color and begin to drop. Avoid mid-summer fertilizing.

The best method of fertilizing is root feeding; that is, make a hole by driving a crowbar approximately 12 to 15 inches into the ground two-thirds of the way from the trunk to the drip line, and pour granular fertilizer into the hole. We recommend that a quality 10-6-4 or 15-5-5 fertilizer be used, 2 pounds per inch of trunk diameter up to 6 inches and 4 pounds per inch of trunk diameter, 6 inches and larger. Root feeding places the fertilizer nearest the active feeder roots of the tree, which are generally in the top 2 feet of soil, extending from the trunk to a circle beyond the spread of the branches. If you have trees with a hard-to-reach bed area, broadcast proper amounts of the fertilizer at the base of the trees.

Flowering trees are fertilized in the same way as shade trees, but you should use 2 pounds of a 5-10-5 or 4-10-4 along with 1 pound of 0-20-0 (superphosphate) per inch of trunk diameter. The addition of this phosphate is essential to promote strong, richly textured buds.

Fertilize pine, spruce, fir, and cedar as you would shade and large flowering trees. Broadcast for smaller varieties, such as juniper, arborvitae, yew, and cypress with ½ pound of 10-6-4 per foot of height or spread, whichever is greater.

Fertilize broad-leaved evergreens with ½ pound of 5-10-5 or 4-10-4 along with ¼ pound of 0-20-0 per foot of height or spread, whichever is greater. Hand-feeding individually and broadcasting are acceptable methods. Because broad-leaved evergreens have shallow roots, you should not cultivate more than 1 inch deep.

If your trees have sparse foliage, small and poorly colored leaves, short annual twig growth, dying branch ends, and noticeable areas of dead wood, they probably need fertilizer.

Shrubs

Ornamental or flowering trees and shrubs are popular in all regions of the country because they add color at various times of the year, grow very quickly, and are generally hardy. There are also many varieties of coniferous evergreen shrubs which contrast beautifully with flowering deciduous shrubs. These relatively small trees and shrubs, ranging in height from 1 to 30 feet, generally represent the horizontal plane in your landscaping design. They can be planted fairly close to the house to enhance small lawn or patio areas and to function as focal points. Shrubs help balance the strong vertical lines created by taller shade trees. Shrubs can also tie all the component parts of a landscape design (lawns, gardens, trees, patios, and flowers) into a unified composition.

Selection Shrubs are generally arranged into groupings consisting of several varieties for a unified, harmonious pattern of seasonal color, size, shape, and texture. Evergreen and deciduous shrubs and flowering trees come in a wide range of sizes, shapes, and colors. Some have brightly colored foliage for two or three seasons, not only in autumn. Some produce beautiful flowers that appeal to both sight and smell. Others remain green and lively during winter months. Some are dense with broad leaves, while others are sparse with needlelike leaves. Fruit produced by shrubs and flowering trees may be edible or provide winter forage for birds and wildlife.

Each shrub should be selected for a specific purpose. Include shrubs that blossom in each season, balance upright shrubs with creeping or spreading varieties, and consider the beauty and desirable characteristics for each shrub. Don't crowd the groupings. Proper spacing will allow each plant to grow and develop, eventually blending together in an attractive, natural manner.

Before purchasing any shrub from the nursery consider the following characteristics:

- coniferous or deciduous; broad-leaf or needle-like
- the approximate controlled height (the average pruned height at which it grows best)
- the hardiness of the variety
- light requirement (full sun or partial shade)
- fruit or flowers
- approximate shape and texture. Deciduous shrubs have a variety of shapes and sizes; evergreen shrubs have one of five basic shapes:
  1—columnar: tall, upright shape (juniper, yew, cedar, arborvitae);
  2—global: round, low-growing shrubs (arborvitae, mugho pine);
  3—spreading: form a screen or hedge when grouped together (juniper, yew);
  4—creeping: low ground cover, usually suitable in hard-to-grow areas (juniper, yew);
  5—pyramidal: triangle-shaped foundation shrub (yew, arborvitae, cypress)
- possible landscape uses
- the autumn foliage color
- watering requirements
- soil requirements
- any special planting requirements

The following charts list several of the primary characteristics of common deciduous and coniferous evergreen shrubs and flowering trees. Determine the plant hardiness from the Hardiness Zone Map.

CONIFEROUS EVERGREEN SHRUBS

Shrub	Height Feet	Growth Habit*	Characteristics/Uses	1	2	3	4	5	6	7	8	9	10
Cypress													
Chamaecyparis lawsoniana elwoodi	5-8	U,C	Use for framing, accents						X	X	X	X	
Chamaecyparis obtusa	5-8	U	Slow growing, use for foreground					X	X	X	X	X	
Chamaecyparis obtusa aurea	5-8	U	Dark green foliage, side plantings					X	X	X	X	X	
Chamaecyparis obtusa compacta	3-4	C	Foundation plantings					X	X	X	X	X	
Chamaecyparis obtusa gracilis	3-5	C,U	Slow growing, distinctive					X	X	X	X	X	
Chamaecyparis obtusa nana	3-4	C	Round, use in shrub grouping					X	X	X	X	X	
Chamaecyparis obtusa pygmaea	1-2	C,S	Creeping small plant				X	X	X	X	X	X	
Chamaecyparis pisifera filifera	6-8	U,S	Bright green foliage		X	X	X	X	X	X	X		
Chamaecyparis pisifera filifera aurea	5-7	U,S	Golden yellow foliage		X	X	X	X	X	X	X		
Chamaecyparis pisifera plumosa	3-9	U	Use as background or windscreen					X	X	X	X	X	
Chamaecyparis pisifera squarrosa minima	1-3	C,S	Very slow grower					X	X	X	X	X	
Juniper													
Juniperus chinensis armstrongii	3-5	S	Can be used as ground cover						X	X	X	X	X
Juniperus chinensis columnaris glauca	12-15	U	Side or background plantings					X	X	X	X	X	
Juniperus chinensis globosa	3-5	C,U	Globelike appearance					X	X	X	X	X	
Juniperus chinensis japonica	4-5	U,S	Good foundation shrub					X	X	X	X	X	
Juniperus chinensis pfitzeriana	4-6	S	Rapid and continuous growth			X	X	X	X	X			
Juniperus chinensis sargentii	1-2	C,S	Good for covering slopes			X	X	X	X	X	X		
Juniperus chinensis torulosa	5-9	U	Attractive, rapid growth								X	X	X
Juniperus communis compressa	3-4	U	Medium hardy, slow growing	X	X	X	X	X	X	X			
Juniperus conferta	1-2	C,S	Prevails along shorelines						X	X	X	X	X
Juniperus horizontalis	1-2	S	Good, level ground cover			X	X	X	X	X			
Juniperus horizontalis plumosa	1-2	C,S	Feathery, light green foliage		X	X	X	X	X	X			
Juniperus procumbens	1-3	S	Very hardy and attractive			X	X	X	X	X			
Juniperus sabina	5-6	U,S	Use in shrub groupings			X	X	X	X	X			
Juniperus sabina tamariscifolia	1-2	C,S	Excellent foreground mat					X	X	X	X	X	
Juniperus squamata meyeri	4-5	U,S	Contributes interest to plantings					X	X	X	X	X	
Juniperus virginiana reptans	2-4	U,S	Hardy, low growing					X	X	X	X	X	
Spruce													
Picea abies nidiformis	4-5	C	Very hardy, slow growing		X	X	X	X	X	X			
Picea abies procumbens	4-5	C,S	Hardy, slow growing		X	X	X	X	X	X			
Picea abies pygmaea	1-3	C	Dense, good for interest areas			X	X	X	X	X	X		
Picea abies remontii	3-4	C,S	Ragged growth, yellow color			X	X	X	X	X	X		
Picea glauca conica	2-3	C,S	Miniature tree of great interest		X	X	X	X	X	X			
Pine													
Pinus mugo	3-4	U,S	Many uses, very hardy		X	X	X	X	X	X	X		
Pinus mugo mughus prostrata	1-2	C,S	Excellent for rock gardens		X	X	X	X	X				
Pinus strobus nana	5-6	U,S	Soft-textured, hardy						X	X	X	X	
Pinus sylvestris nana glauca	5-7	U	Excellent near patio or pool						X	X	X		
Yew													
Taxus baccata adpressa	4-5	C,S	Good foundation shrub, hardy						X	X	X	X	X
Taxus baccata fastigiata	7-10	C,S	Slow growing, dense, beautiful							X	X	X	
Taxus baccata repandens	2-4	C,S	Informally sprawling, dense							X	X	X	
Taxus canadensis	3-4	S	Hardy, straggly, low growing						X	X	X	X	
Taxus cuspidata densa	3-4	U	Rich, dark green foliage						X	X	X	X	
Taxus cuspidata nana	3-4	C,U	Small Japanese yew						X	X	X	X	
Taxus cuspidata minima	1-2	C,S	Creeper, use on small slopes						X	X	X	X	
Arborvitae													
Thuja koraiensis	4-10	C,U	Shrub-type arborvitae					X	X	X	X		
Thuja occidentalis ellwangeriana aurea	3-4	C,U	Golden sheen, heavy foliage					X	X	X	X		
Thuja occidentalis fastigiata	8-18	C,U	Perfect hedge or windscreen					X	X	X	X		
Thuja occidentalis globosa	3-4	C,U	Forms dense globe, formal						X	X	X	X	
Thuja occidentalis pumila	1-2	C,U	Excellent for small interest areas						X	X	X	X	
Thuja orientalis aurea nana	2-3	C,U	Hardy accent or special purpose shrub							X	X	X	X
Thuja orientalis beverleyensis	6-7	C,U	Medium hardy, use for framing							X	X	X	X
Thuja orientalis conspicua	4-5	C,U	Strong character, golden color							X	X	X	X
Hemlock													
Tsuga canadensis nana	1-2	S	Very hardy, good in rock gardens					X	X	X	X	X	
Tsuga canadensis pendula	2-3	C,U	Slow-growing, well-formed						X	X	X	X	

*(U)pright, (C)ompact, (S)preading

FLOWERING TREES AND SHRUBS

Tree	Height Feet	Growth Rate	Characteristics	Month of Bloom	Flower Color	1	2	3	4	5	6	7	8	9	10
Flowering Almond	3-8	Mod.	Very cold hardy	May	Pink, white				X	X	X	X	X	X	X
Andromeda	5-9	Slow	Somewhat hardy, light tolerant	April	White				X	X	X	X	X	X	X
Azalea	3-6	Mod.	Good foundation plant	Varied	Varied						X	X	X	X	X
Barberry	3-6	Mod.	Thorns, red leaves and berries	April-May	Yellow			X	X	X	X	X	X	X	
Beauty Bush	5-8	Mod. to fast	Medium hardy, easy to grow	June	Pink, yellow						X	X	X	X	X
Bottlebrush	5-20	Fast	Requires sun and warmth	May	Red								X	X	X
Buckthorn	8-15	Mod. to fast	Very hardy, black fruit	May	Green	X	X	X	X	X	X				
Black Cherry	20-35	Mod. to fast	Birds attracted by fruit	April-May	White, pink				X	X	X	X		X	
Cornelian Cherry	10-20	Mod. to fast	Birds attracted by fruit	April-May	Pink				X	X	X	X	X		
Japanese Cherry	12-25	Mod.	Very beautiful	April-May	Pink, white						X	X	X		X
Sargent Cherry	25-40	Mod.	Full sun	April-May	Pink				X	X	X	X	X		
Cotoneaster	8-10	Mod.	Perfect for small lot, hardy	May	Pink						X	X	X	X	
Crabapples	10-40	Mod.	Fruit can be messy, many varieties	May	White, pink	X	X	X	X	X	X	X	X	X	X
Currant	3-8	Mod. to fast	Easy to grow, somewhat hardy	May	Pink	X	X	X	X	X					
Dogwood	10-25	Mod.	Horizontal branching	May-June	Cream				X	X	X	X	X	X	X
American Elder	10-15	Fast	Adaptable to several climates	June	White	X	X	X	X	X	X	X			
Forsythia	5-8	Mod.	Hardy, easy to grow	April	Yellow	X	X	X	X	X	X				
Gardenia	3-5	Mod.	Spreading, fragrant flowers	September	White								X	X	X
Golden Chain	9-20	Mod. to fast	Requires warm climate	May-June	Yellow							X	X	X	X
Hawthorn	15-25	Mod.	Open branching, autumn color	May	Varied					X	X	X	X	X	
Hibiscus	5-12	Slow	Evergreen, heavy foliage	June	Varied								X	X	X
Honeysuckle	8-15	Mod.	Adaptable to poor soil conditions	May-June	Varied			X	X	X	X	X	X		
Hydrangea	5-8	Mod.	Grows in partial shade	June-Sept.	Varied				X	X	X	X	X	X	
Lilac	10-25	Mod. to fast	Magnificent, fragrant flowers	May	Varied		X	X	X	X	X	X	X	X	
Mexican-Orange	4-7	Slow to Mod.	Needs mild, warm climate	May-June	White								X	X	X
Mock Orange	5-18	Mod.	Somewhat hardy, fragrant flowers	May	White				X	X	X	X	X	X	X
Myrtle	8-20	Slow	Needs mild, warm climate	May	Varied								X	X	X
Oleander	8-15	Mod.	Poisonous leaves	May-Aug.	Pink, red							X	X	X	X
Japanese Pagoda	30-60	Mod. to fast	Tolerates many soil conditions	August	Yellow, white				X	X	X	X	X	X	X
Peach	15-25	Mod.	Produces excellent fruit	May	Cream						X	X	X	X	X
Pear	10-20	Mod.	Produces excellent fruit	May	White				X	X	X	X	X		
Plum	10-20	Fast	Somewhat hardy, good fruit	May	Pale blue				X	X	X	X	X	X	X
Privet	5-12	Mod.	Very versatile in use	July	White						X	X	X	X	X
Quince	2-8	Mod.	Best used for accents	March	Crimson						X	X	X	X	
Rhododendron	2-25	Mod. to fast	Easy to grow, popular shrub	May-June	Varied						X	X	X	X	X
Rosemary	3-7	Mod.	Medium hardy, use for accents	May-June	Blue							X	X	X	X
Snowball	8-15	Mod.	Very hardy, graceful	May	White		X			X	X	X	X		
Snowberry	3-8	Fast	Hardy, clustered flowers	May	Pink				X	X	X	X	X	X	
Sumac	5-10	Fast	Very hardy, beautiful red foliage	May	White	X	X	X	X	X	X	X			
Summersweet	3-8	Mod.	Beautiful late-blooming shrub	July-Aug.	Cream						X	X	X	X	

Planting Depending on whether you buy a small tree or shrub in a container, wrapped in burlap or in bare-root form, the techniques described for planting shade trees should be followed.

A hedge has many advantages over a constructed fence or barrier. It is more natural, visually pleasing, and harbors birds and wildlife. Hedges can be allowed to grow naturally or can be tightly and formally trimmed. Formal hedges require more work but can be quite beautiful. Steps for planting a hedge include:

1. Dig a trench 12 inches deep and 10 inches wide. Mix composted manure with the soil taken from the trench (1 pound of manure per running foot of trench).
2. Place the hedge plants on a mound of prepared soil about 12 inches apart, except for the barberry type which should be spaced 24 inches apart.
3. Backfill around the plants with the remaining prepared soil, firm around roots, and water thoroughly.
4. For privet-type hedges, remove 75 percent of the top growth; for the barberry, remove only 15 percent of the growth. Frequent pruning of the plant will make it grow dense rather than tall.

Pruning Shrubs and flowering trees are pruned for the same reasons as larger shade trees.

Fertilizing Coniferous needlelike and broad-leaved shrubs should be fertilized like their taller shade tree counterparts as described earlier.

Fertilize flowering deciduous shrubs with ½ pound of 5-10-5 or 4-10-4 per one foot of height or spread, whichever is greater, mixed with ¼ pound of 0-20-0 to increase flower production. If you prefer not to root-feed these shrubs (depending on size), you can work the fertilizer into the top inch of soil around the base of the shrub. Caution: If any of the fertilizer gets on the plant, it may burn the leaves.

Pests on Trees and Shrubs

This chapter explains how to recognize and control the more common insects and mites that attack trees and shrubs in widespread areas of the United States. The homeowner will find that the insecticides recommended for control are, with few exceptions, readily available and provide a wide range of uses. The sprays are easy to prepare, and if directions are followed they can be used safely.

If you need additional, more specific information, write to your local extension agent, your Cooperative Extension Service, or to the U.S. Department of Agriculture, Washington, D.C. 20250. Include your return address and ZIP code. If you cannot identify the insects that are damaging your plants, shrubs, or trees, take specimens of the insects (in a small bottle of rubbing alcohol) to your local extension agent or Cooperative Extension Service.

Insecticide Sprays

Few sprays come ready to use on the trees and shrubs. It is usually necessary to prepare a spray by mixing a wettable powder or an emulsifiable concentrate with water. These materials contain different percentages of an active ingredient (different strengths). The table, "Insecticide Spray Formulations and Mixing Proportions," shows how to mix sprays in the strengths recommended for control of insects in home plantings. If you use a material in which the percentage of active ingredient differs from that shown in the table, mix proportionately more or less of it with the water. If you use a wettable powder, stir it vigorously in a small amount of water to make a smooth paste, or slurry. Add this to the full amount of water and stir until completely mixed. When applying wettable-powder sprays, shake the applicator frequently to keep the powder from settling to the bottom of the spray chamber. If you use an emulsifiable concentrate, shake the container thoroughly before measuring out the amount needed for the spray mixture.

Use of Pesticides

Pesticide use is governed by a federal law which is administered by the Environmental Protection Agency. This law requires manufacturers to register pesticides and makes it illegal for people to use them except in accordance with the instructions on the label. You may, if you wish, use less of any pesticide than the maximum amount the instruc-

INSECTICIDE SPRAY FORMULATIONS AND MIXING PROPORTIONS

Insecticide	Formulation[1]	Amount of formulation to mix with 1 gallon of water[2]
Azinphosmethyl	12.4% EC	3 t.
Bacillus thuringiensis	16,000 IUP/mg	½ to 2 t.
Carbaryl	50% WP	2 level T.
Diazinon	50% WP	2 level t.
Dicofol[3]	35% WP or	1½ T.
	18.5% EC	1 to 2 t.
Endosulfan	50% WP or	4 t.
	25% EC	1 T.
Lindane	20% EC	1½ T.
Malathion	25% WP or	1 T.
	57% EC	1 t.
Methoxychlor	25% EC	3 T.
Mineral Oil	100% EC	10 T.
Oxydemetonmethyl	25% EC	1½ t.
Trichlorfon	40% EC	1 T.

[1]WP = wettable power; EC = emulsifiable concentrate.
[2]If the available formulation contains more or less of the indicated active ingredient, mix proportionately more or less of it with 1 gallon of water.
[3]Dicofol is commonly found on the label with other active ingredients. In these instances, use dosage recommended on the label.

tions permit. Be sure the pesticide comes in contact only with plants or areas you intend to spray, and be sure to spray the pesticides uniformly.

Special Precautions Diazinon, endosulfan, lindane, and oxydemetonmethyl can be absorbed directly through the skin in harmful quantities. When working with these pesticides in any form, take extra care not to let them come in contact with the skin. Wear protective clothing and use respiratory devices as directed on the label. The other pesticides mentioned can be used without special protective clothing or respiratory devices if they are in dilute form.

- Carbaryl—Do not use carbaryl on Boston ivy as injury may result.
- Diazinon—Do not use diazinon on certain chrysanthemum, ferns, poinsettia, hibiscus, papaya, pilea, and gardenia because plant injury may occur.
- Dicofol—Do not use dicofol on Chinese holly or Canaerti juniper or injury may result.

- Endosulfan—Do not apply endosulfan to white birch or American redbud because it may injure foliage. Do not apply endosulfan to Anderson yew because it may cause needle drop.
- Malathion—Do not apply malathion to ferns, hickory, viburnum, lantana, Crassula and Canaerti juniper, Boston pteris, maidenhair ferns, petunias, small leaf spiraea, white pine, and maples because injury may result. Under extreme heat, drought, and disease conditions the emulsifiable concentrates of malathion may cause slight damage to elms.
- Trichlorfon—Do not apply trichlorfon to certain varieties of carnations, hydrangeas, and zinnias because it may injure foliage.

General Pests

Although there are a host of insects that attack trees and shrubs, three cause the most damage—mites, scales, and bores.

SIGNS OF TREE INSECTS

Signs	Insects
Leaves chewed and eventually devoured	Caterpillars, beetles, earwigs
Leaves appear to have small holes throughout	Japanese beetles, pear slug (worm)
Leaves tunneled along veins	Leaf miners (larvae of small fly)
Leaves rolled to protect feeding insects	Aphids, some caterpillars

Note: Regular seasonal spraying with a malathion-lindane solution protects against all of the above insects.

Mites The most common of insects, mites, are only about 1/50 inch long and impossible to detect with the human eye. They can be colorless, tan, red, or purple. Mites attack the leaves of the plant by drawing out the juices through tiny puncture holes, which cause the leaves to become yellow and ultimately to fall from the plant. The presence of a great many mites is indicated by the white silklike web they leave on the underside of the leaves. Treatment with a malathion-lindane spray or Isotox, an Ortho product, early in the spring will reduce the chances of infestation. If damage has already started, spray twice a week until the mites are gone and no further damage is evident.

Scales Scales are tiny growthlike insects that attach themselves and look like tiny bumps on the stem of a plant. In warm summer months their young hatch and move about invisibly while feeding on plants. In the early spring, while the insect remains dormant, apply an oil-base insecticide. A malathion-lindane spray can be used to control the young.

Bores Bores are classified as roundheaded or flatheaded, and there are many varieties of each. They do more damage to birch, apple, and dogwood trees and lilacs than any other insect. Adult bores (moths or beetles) lay their eggs just under the surface of the outer bark. When the young hatch, they drill or bore into the cambium layer or lifeline of the tree. If unheeded, the bores will feed on the cambium layer until it is severed, and eventually cause the death of the limb or entire tree. At the first sign of damage, cut off and burn all infected parts.

Some insect pests attack a wide variety of trees and shrubs. The following information outlines their life history and suggests methods to control them.

Aphids
Description—Several species: tiny; light green, dark green, or black; soft bodied; winged or wingless, cluster on stems and under leaves.

Damage—Cause leaves to curl and thicken, turn yellow, and die. Leaves often sticky from honeydew produced by aphids.

Distribution—Continental United States.

Control—Apply malathion or oxydemetonmethyl as soon as aphids appear; or wash the aphids off the plants with a soap and water solution applied under fairly high pressure.

Cankerworms
Description—Two species: spring cankerworm and fall cankerworm. Adults: brown moths with stripes on wings. Larvae: brown to green looping or measuring worms.

Damage—Feed on leaves and defoliate plants.

Distribution—East of the Rocky Mountains, California.

Control—Apply methoxychlor, carbaryl, or *Bacillus thuringiensis* when caterpillars first appear in the spring. A band of tanglefoot placed around the trunk of the tree 2 to 4 feet above the ground will help to reduce infestation.

Casebearers and Bagworms
Description—Several species. Adults: small, gray moths. Larvae: brown to dark brown. Can grow as long as 1½ inches and are found on leaves in conspicuous, spindle- or cigar-shaped cases or bags.

Damage—Larvae eat leaves and buds.

Distribution—Continental United States.

Control—To control bagworms, apply diazinon, *Bacillus thuringiensis*, malathion or trichlorfon. Remove bags and destroy them.

Gypsy Moth
Description—Female: light-buff color; irregular, darker markings across wings. Heavy bodied; cannot fly very long. Lays eggs in masses up to 1 inch long covered with a coating of hair. Eggs are deposited in July but do not hatch until May. Male: dark

brown; small bodied; strong flyer. Larvae: suspended by wind. Caterpillars are dark with long, rather stiff brown tufts of hair projecting from sides of body and yellow stripes down back. Up to 2 inches long. Blue and red dots arranged in two rows down the back.

Damage—Strip trees of foliage often causing death.

Distribution—Northeastern United States.

Control—Apply *Bacillus thuringiensis*, carbaryl, or trichlorfon when caterpillars first appear. Reduce infestations by destroying egg masses and by banding the tree trunks with sticky material.

Japanese Beetle

Description—Adult: shiny green; reddish-brown outer wings; oval; about ½ inch long and ¼ inch wide. Larva: white, brown head; up to 1 inch long.

Damage—Adult attacks foliage. Larva feeds on roots of grasses and other plants.

Distribution—Southern Maine and south as far as Georgia and westward into Kentucky, Illinois, Michigan, and Missouri.

Control—To control adults, apply carbaryl, methoxychlor, or malathion to infested foliage.

Small trees and shrubs, especially roses, can be protected from injury by covering them with plastic or cloth netting as soon as beetles begin to appear.

Lace Bugs

Description—Several species. Adults: lacy wings with brown and black markings; ⅛ inch long. Nymphs: spiny; colorless at first, later become black.

Damage—Nymphs and adults suck sap from underside of leaves causing gray, stippled appearance on the upper surface.

Distribution—Continental United States.

Control—Apply malathion or diazinon when lace bugs are first noticed. Adults migrate from neighboring plants; repeat treatment in 10 days and again several weeks later.

Leafminers

Description—Several species. Adults: small moths, beetles, or flies. Larvae: small worms found inside leaves in irregular-shaped tunnels.

Damage—Deform, cause dead areas on leaves.

Distribution—Continental United States.

Control—Apply diazinon or oxydemetonmethyl when damage is evident. Destroy the young larvae in the leaves to prevent subsequent attacks by later generations.

Mealybugs

Description—Several species. Females: soft, oval, segmented body covered with a white, powdery wax. White, cottony filament covers masses of eggs behind female. About ¼ inch long. Adult male: winged, does not feed. Crawlers (young): flattened, oval, light-yellow, smooth bodies, ⅛ to ¼ inch long, present in early spring and in early summer.

Damage—Female sucks juices from roots, stems, and leaves of plants dwarfing their growth. Secretes honeydew-like material.

Distribution—Continental United States.

Control—Apply malathion when crawlers are active; repeat in 10 days if necessary.

Tent Caterpillars and Webworms

Description—Several species. Adults: white to brown moths; active near lights. Larvae: hairy caterpillars; up to 2 inches long; construct tents of webbing on branches.

Damage—Feed on leaves, can defoliate trees.

Distribution—Continental United States.

Control—For tent caterpillars, apply malathion or methoxychlor, and for fall webworm on ornamental trees, apply methoxychlor when webs are first noticed. Webs with worms can be removed with a pole or brush.

Whiteflies

Description—Several species. Adults: wedge-shaped; white-winged; 1/16 inch long; fly in a cloud when disturbed. Nymphs: oval; pale green; waxy threads or spines; motionless on underside of leaves; usually present in large numbers.

Damage—Adults and nymphs suck sap from leaves which become pale yellow, sticky with honeydew, and blackened with sooty mold.

Distribution—Continental United States.

Control—Apply malathion or oxydemetonmethyl once a week for 2 or 3 weeks. Concentrate coverage on underside of leaves.

Whitemarked Tussock Moth

Description—Adult gray moth: wingspread 1¼ inches. Dark, wavy bands across wings. Female: wings are stubby; cannot fly; body stout, hairy, dirty white. Larvae: yellow and black, hairy, striped caterpillars up to 1¾ inches long. Easily recognized by four tufts of short, white, erect hairs on the back and by two bright red spots on the back.

Damage—Leaves are skeletonized by caterpillars.

Distribution—Eastern United States and Canada, westward to Colorado and British Columbia. Less troublesome in the South.

Control—Apply carbaryl when larvae appear in spring; repeat treatment for later broods.

Growing Ground Covers and Vines

Ground covers are an ideal finishing touch at the base of shrubs in a foundation planting. Vines can help decorate a lamppost, a fence, or any vertical object.

Ground covers include a wide range of low-growing plants. Common uses include:

- Cover bare areas of ground.
- Prevent erosion of the soil.
- Give variety in the yard or garden.
- Regulate foot traffic in the yard or garden when used as edging for pathways.
- Tie together unrelated shrubs and flower beds in the landscape.

Many kinds of annuals or perennials may serve as ground covers. Broad-leaved evergreens are the best, but conifers and deciduous plants also are suitable.

Plants can be propagated at home, but home propagation is slow. Usually plants purchased from a nursery grow better because they are already established in containers and ready for planting.

Ground covers range in size from plants as short as grass to shrubs 3 or more feet high. Creeping and dwarf lilyturf, for example, cover the ground like grass, but cotoneaster and juniper depend on the matting of stems and leaves or the interlocking of branches to cover the ground. Ground covers usually maintain themselves with a minimum of care once they become established.

Because the thick, spreading growth of ground covers helps to delay the alternate freezing and thawing of the soil, these plants may grow better in cold climates than most upright plants. This is especially true in areas where snow covers the ground in winter or the planting is mulched with pine needles, straw, or branches. Ground covers are least adapted to areas of low rainfall and low humidity.

Plants described in this section and the charts are keyed to numbered hardiness zones shown on the map in the tree chapter. Soil type, rainfall, summer temperatures, and other conditions also govern whether a plant can thrive without unusual attention. Many times these factors can change within ten miles.

The following chart lists basic information for common varieties of ground cover.

GROUND COVERS

Name	Height (Inches)	Description	1	2	3	4	5	6	7	8	9	10
Barrenwort	8-12	dense foliage, excellent for underplanting					X	X	X	X		
Bearberry	7-12	fine-textured, dark foliage, red fruit, hardy	X	X	X	X	X	X	X	X	X	
Bugleweed	4-8	creeping perennial, grows rapidly					X	X	X	X		
Capeweed	2-4	grows in poor soils, grasslike, pink flowers									X	X
Cinquefoil	7-12	yellow flowers, creeping, carpetlike					X	X	X	X		
Coralberry	15-30	thrives in poor soil, good for taller cover					X	X	X	X	X	
Cotoneaster	6-30	perfect for banks, rough areas, accents					X	X	X	X	X	
Cowberry	8-12	good in acid soils, pink flowers, red fruit				X	X	X	X	X		
Creeping Thyme	1-3	good for edging or around stepping stones					X	X	X	X	X	X
Crown Vetch	12-24	perfect for dry, steep slopes, spreading				X	X	X	X	X		
Day Lily	8-10	thrives along banks, blooms all season			X	X	X	X	X	X	X	X
Dichondra	1-2	runnerlike stems, spreads rapidly									X	X
Dwarf Holly Grape	6-10	grows rapidly in most soils						X	X	X	X	X
English Ivy	6-8	coarse foliage, dense cover, fast spreading					X	X	X	X	X	
Germander	5-10	woody perennial, excellent border						X	X	X	X	X
Goldmoss Stonecrop	2-4	good for dry soils, rocky areas, creeping					X	X	X	X	X	X
Ground Ivy	1-3	matlike, requires confinement				X	X	X	X	X		
Heather	7-12	creeping, pink or purple flowers						X	X	X	X	X
Honeysuckle	12-24	climbing fragrant vine, prune yearly						X	X	X	X	X
Ice Plant	5-12	good for banks or roadsides									X	X
Japanese Holly	12-24	evergreen, slow growing, needs semishade						X	X	X	X	X
Japanese Spurge	4-6	spreads rapidly, ideal for underplanting						X	X	X	X	
Juniper, Creeping	7-12	excellent evergreen covering, spreading			X	X	X	X	X	X	X	X
Juniper, Japanese	12-18	upright shrub, many landscape uses				X	X	X	X	X		

Name	Height (Feet)	Description	1	2	3	4	5	6	7	8	9	10
Juniper, Sargents	12-18	good for use around rocks, hardy			X	X	X	X	X			
Juniper, Tamarix	12-18	evergreen shrub, requires semishade				X	X	X	X	X		
Memorial Rose	6-12	large white flowers, salt tolerant					X	X	X	X	X	X
Moss Sandwort	1-3	mosslike perennial, good for small areas			X	X	X	X	X	X	X	X
Periwinkle	6-8	easily propagated, blue or purple flowers					X	X	X	X	X	X
St. Johnswort	9-12	grows well in sandy soil and semishade						X	X	X	X	X
Sand Strawberry	4-6	spreads rapidly, grows well in most soils						X	X	X	X	X
Sarcococca	30-48	glossy, leathery leaves, control required						X	X	X	X	X
Sunrose	5-12	yellow flowers, suitable for edging					X	X	X	X	X	
Trailing Arbutus	7-12	good in sun or partial shade, pink flowers	X	X	X	X	X	X	X	X	X	
Wandering Jew	6-9	good in shade, tender, good ground cover										X
Weeping Lantana	12-18	trailing shrub, many varieties and colors								X	X	X
Wintercreeper	12-18	fast growth, spreads rapidly, evergreen					X	X	X	X	X	

VINES

Name	Height (Feet)	Description	Zone									
			1	2	3	4	5	6	7	8	9	10
Allamanda	25-40	vigorous growth, large yellow flowers								X	X	X
Boston Ivy	15-30	brilliant autumn foliage, good on surfaces					X	X	X	X	X	
Clematis	5-25	pink or violet flowers, good on trellis					X	X	X	X	X	
Climbing Roses	5-15	see rose chapter for more specific information				X	X	X	X	X	X	
Creeping Fig	10-50	creates fascinating patterns									X	X
English Ivy	8-50	hardy, self-attaching, widely used			X	X	X	X	X	X	X	
Jade	5-15	strong growing ornamental vine								X	X	X
Jasmine	7-12	very fragrant flowers, strong climber						X	X	X	X	X
Morning Glory	5-15	beautiful flowers in a combination of colors								X	X	X
Trumpet Vine	15-30	hardy, densely growing, needs support					X	X	X	X	X	
Wisteria	15-40	dense foliage, very fragrant flowers					X	X	X	X	X	X

Planting

The selection of ground covers and planting methods vary from region to region. Ground covers are generally used in areas where conditions are bad for plant growth, such as steep slopes, dense shade, dryness, poor drainage, or exposure to wind. Once ground covers are established, they usually need little care but the site must be prepared thoroughly before planting.

Dig the soil at least 6 inches deep. Spread 2 to 3 inches of organic material such as peat, well-rotted manure, or leaf mold over the ground and spade it into the soil.

On uneven ground where the entire area cannot be worked, dig individual planting holes. Dig these deep enough so you can backfill partially with soil mixed with organic material before you set the plants. Use topsoil for the rest of the refill.

Plant most slopes and banks with ground covers. Low banks 2 to 4 feet high can be planted without any additional preparation, but you should build retaining walls at the foot of steep slopes to reduce the slope and help prevent erosion. Sloping areas are usually dry so you must select plants that will tolerate periodic drought. Usually large, vigorous plants such as junipers or cotoneasters are grown on slopes.

Use a fertilizer on the planting site when you prepare the soil. Follow recommendations generally used in your area. Fertilizer needs vary according to soil types in various parts of the country. Spade the fertilizer into the soil.

Except under extreme conditions, you should not alter the soil pH for specific plants. Generally, you should choose plants adapted to existing pH conditions. If soils are extremely acid, you can improve them by using 10 to 25 pounds of dolomitic limestone per 100 square feet.

Although you can plant ground covers anytime during the growing season, early spring is the best time in most localities.

The following chart shows the area that approximately 100 plants will cover when set at various distances apart. For example, if you set the plants 4 inches apart, 100 plants will cover about 11 square feet.

Planting Distance (Inches)	Area Covered (Square Feet)
4	11
6	25
3	44
10	70
12	100
18	225
24	400
36	900
48	1600

When you plant ground covers, space them so they will cover the site as quickly as possible. You may put small plants like bugleweed as close as 4 to 6 inches apart. Set such large plants as juniper or cotoneaster as much as 4 feet apart. Closer planting will cover the ground more rapidly, but the cost of additional plants may be prohibitive.

Care of Plants

A well-established ground cover planting usually needs little maintenance. Fertilizing, mulching, weeding, and watering are the main requirements.

Fertilize the plants in winter and again in early spring. To avoid burning the foliage, scatter a pelleted form of commercial fertilizer over the planting when the foliage is dry.

Ground covers are slower than grass in covering bare ground. Consequently, weeds are likely to grow, especially the first year. A mulch of wood chips, straw, or other organic refuse will control most weeds as well as retain moisture in the soil. Pull weeds by hand if they break through the mulch.

Do not dig around the plants. Digging breaks the roots and promotes germination of weed seeds.

Do not rely on summer rainfall to keep your ground covers watered. Water on a regular schedule throughout the growing season, particularly during dry weather. Allow the water to penetrate deeply into the soil, but do not water so heavily that the soil becomes soggy. Water again when the soil is dry to the touch and the tips of the plants wilt slightly at midday. During the winter months, water the plants thoroughly when the weather is dry and the temperature is above freezing.

In cold climates with no permanent snow cover, plantings in direct sunlight may need protection during the winter months to prevent thawing of plant tissues. Direct sunlight can cause permanent damage. Lay conifer branches or burlap over the beds to protect the plants. If the plants heave out of the soil in cold weather, push them back immediately. Do not wait until spring.

Ground covers usually need pruning only to remove dead wood and keep the planting in bounds.

Ground covers will show winter injury as do other plants. Evergreen plants, for example, suffer considerable damage when the foliage has been burned following an extremely dry winter. You can shear such plantings or individually prune out damaged branches.

Plantings of juniper may be so badly winter damaged that soil areas become bare. When this happens, you should replant bare areas rather than wait until the old planting fills in the gaps.

You can reduce winter damage by covering the plants with a waterproofing spray. These sprays are available at garden supply stores. If you spray plants in the fall, they will retain the waterproof cover for most of the winter months. You also should spray plants when you transplant them.

Propagation

The propagation of most ground covers is simple. Making cuttings and dividing are the most common methods. Annuals and some perennials can be seeded outdoors or seeded in flats and transplanted outdoors. Most of the larger plants such as junipers or cotoneasters are established from plants purchased from a nursery.

Making Cuttings Many plants can be propagated from either tip or root cuttings. Generally, tip cuttings are easier to propagate. Before you take your cuttings, prepare a tray of peat pots. Use a soil mix of two parts sand, one part soil, and one part peat moss. Make tip cuttings 3 to 6 inches long. Treat the base of each cutting with a root stimulant. Rooting powders are sold in three strengths. Be sure to follow the directions on the can for the correct dosage. Leave all foliage on the cuttings except the part that you put below the soil line. Insert one cutting in each peat pot. Water thoroughly.

Place the tray of tip cuttings in a lightly shaded area. Cover with a sheet of plastic. Check regularly to make sure the cuttings do not dry out. The cuttings should start rooting in ten to thirty days. You can test them by pulling gently to see if they are secure. When rooting starts, make holes in the plastic sheet to let air in and to increase the exposure of the cuttings to the air. This will harden the cuttings. Every few days make new holes, or make the holes larger. Finally, remove the cover. Allow the cuttings to grow. Pinch back their tips ten days after the cover is removed to promote branching. Transplant the rooted cuttings to a freshly prepared bed in midsummer.

Dig root cuttings in late summer. Select pencil-size roots and cut them into 4-inch sections. Put each piece in a peat pot. Water thoroughly. Keep the peat pots of root cuttings in a cold frame. Transplant them the next spring.

Dividing Divide mature clumps of ground covers. Select only vigorous side shoots, the outer part of the clump. This is the part that will grow best. Discard the center of the clump. Divide the plant into clumps of three to five shoots each. Be careful not to overdivide because too small a clump will not give much cover the first year after replanting.

The best time to divide ground covers is late summer or fall in southern areas and in spring in northern areas.

Roses

Roses are probably the most popular of all garden flowers because of their beauty, fragrance, and adaptability. They can be grown in every part of the country and are used for many decorative purposes.

Many varieties of roses are available; ask your nurseryman to help you choose the plants that will give you the desired effect in your landscaping design. Roses are available for planting on lawns and in borders, for growing on arbors and trellises or as specimen tree roses, and for use as bedding plants, as hedges, and as a source of cut flowers. New varieties, developed by plant breeders, are introduced each year. These new varieties are available in a wide range of colors, forms, and fragrances.

For success in growing garden roses follow these tips:

- Buy vigorous plants from a reputable local nursery, retail store, or mail-order nursery.
- Select a planting site that receives at least 6 hours of sunshine daily.
- Set plants in well-prepared beds.
- Water them frequently.
- Cut flowers from the plant without damaging the remaining parts of the plant.
- Prune the plants every year.
- Spray or dust regularly to prevent insect or disease damage.
- Protect the plants from winter injury.

Though some kinds of wild roses are very desirable in natural landscaping and may be found in many gardens, they are gradually being replaced by named varieties which flower throughout the gardening season.

Roses are separated into three main classes—bush roses, climbing roses, and tree roses—by their habits of growth. Full-grown bush roses are 1 to 3 feet high and require no support. Climbing roses produce long canes and must be provided with some kind of support. Tree roses can grow to a height of 6 feet and make a superb focal point for your design.

Bush Roses

The bush roses are grouped into types according to their flowering habit, winter hardiness, and other traits. The most popular types of bush roses are hybrid tea, floribunda, grandiflora, polyantha, hybrid perpetual, shrub, old-fashioned, and miniature.

Hybrid Teas Hybrid teas are the so-called monthly or everblooming roses. They are more widely grown than all other types of roses combined. When the word "rose" is used, it generally suggests a hybrid tea variety.

Mature hybrid tea rosebushes are 2 to 6 feet high, depending on variety and pruning frequency. The flowers vary from singles, which have but one row of petals, to doubles with many rows. In general, the buds are pointed and long and the flowers are borne one to a stem or in clusters of three to five. Hybrid tea varieties are available in a wide range of colors, including pure white, and many shades of red, yellow, pink, and orange. All varieties are good for cutting.

Most hybrid teas have some fragrance. This characteristic, however, is variable. When fragrance is present, it is usually most intense in the early morning.

Most hybrid teas are winter hardy in areas where the winter temperatures do not often go below zero, but varieties differ in cold resistance. In sections where winters are severe, practically all varieties need protection.

Floribundas Floribunda roses bear their flowers in clusters, and the individual blooms of many of them closely resemble hybrid teas. They are increasing in popularity, especially for bed plantings where large numbers of flowers are wanted. Floribundas will tolerate more neglect than any other type of rose, with the possible exception of some of the shrub species.

Grandifloras Grandiflora roses resemble hybrid teas in type of bloom—single on long stems—and in hardiness. Though the flowers are somewhat smaller than those of hybrid teas, grandifloras bloom more abundantly. The flowers are good for cutting.

Polyanthas Flowers of polyantha roses are smaller than those of the grandifloras and are borne in rather large clusters. The clusters are similar in form and in size of individual flowers to many of the climbing roses, to which the polyanthas are closely related. The polyanthas are hardy and may be grown in many areas where hybrid teas are difficult to grow. Their chief use is in bed plantings or in borders with perennials. They are excellent for mass plantings. They tend to flower only once a year in early summer.

Hybrid Perpetuals Hybrid perpetuals are the June roses of yesteryear's garden. Their flowers are

Bush roses in a flower bed.

Climbing roses on a post and rail fence.

large. Generally they lack the form of hybrid teas.

Before the development of modern hybrid teas, hybrid perpetual roses were very popular. As their name indicates, they are considered as everblooming types, although most of them do not bear continuously through the growing season as do hybrid teas. They usually develop large, vigorous bushes if given good cultural care and proper pruning. They are very hardy and stand low winter temperatures without protection.

Shrub Roses Shrub roses are actually a miscellaneous group of wild species, hybrids, and varieties that develop a large, dense type of growth that is useful in general landscape work. They are hardy in all sections of the country. While their flowers do not equal those of other types of roses in size or form, many bear very attractive seedpods in the fall. They have fine-textured foliage, and some are quite useful for hedges or screen plantings.

Old-Fashioned Roses Old-fashioned roses include the varieties and species that were popular in Colonial gardens. Though the flowers of old-fashioned roses are not as attractive as those of newer varieties, they usually are much more fragrant. These roses are all very hardy, require little care, and furnish an abundance of flowers in June.

Miniature Roses Miniature rose plants, including leaves and flowers, are very small; for some varieties the maximum height is about 6 inches. They are available in all the colors, forms, and fragrances of the large-flowered plants. Miniatures are used mostly for rock gardens, edging beds, and borders. They also may be grown in containers in a window or under fluorescent lights.

Climbing Roses

Climbing roses include all varieties that produce long canes and require support to hold the plants up off the ground. They are often trained on fences or trellises, and some are used without support to cover banks and aid in holding the soil in place. Climbing roses are hardy. They are becoming more popular with the development of finer varieties.

Climbing roses, like bush roses, are grouped into several types. There is much overlapping among types, and some varieties could qualify under several.

Ramblers Rambler roses are very rapid growers. They sometimes develop canes as long as 20 feet in one season. The flowers are small—less than 2 inches across—and are borne in dense clusters. The plants flower only once during a season and on wood that was produced the preceding year. The foliage is glossy and the plants are very hardy; but, unfortunately, many varieties are very susceptible to mildew.

Large-Flowered Climbers Large-flowered climbers grow slowly in comparison with ramblers. They are often trained on posts or some other type of support and may require rather heavy annual pruning to keep them in bounds. These roses are well adapted to small gardens where they may be trained against a wall, fence, or small trellis. When the plants are grown well, the flowers are rather large and are useful for cutting.

Everblooming Climbers Everblooming climbers usually bear an abundance of flowers in early summer. After this period of heavy bloom, the plants produce a few scattered flowers until fall. Then if growing conditions are favorable, the plants again may bear heavily.

Plant breeders are improving this type of rose rapidly. Some everblooming climbers are available that bloom as continuously as hybrid teas and are more winter hardy.

Climbing Hybrid Teas Climbing hybrid tea roses have originated as seedlings and as chance sports (mutations) of bush varieties. When a bush hybrid tea produces a cane that has the climbing character, the new type of plant is usually given the same name as the bush variety from which it originated.

The climbing forms of hybrid teas, in general, do not bloom as continuously as their bush parents. The flowers, foliage, and other characteristics, however, are usually identical. The climbing hybrid teas are just as susceptible to winter injury as the bush forms.

Climbing Polyanthas and Floribundas These types, like the climbing hybrid teas, originated as sports and seedlings from polyanthas and floribundas. The flowers of these sports are generally identical with the bush forms from which they originated, and they also are fairly continuous in blooming. They are hardier than the climbing hybrid teas, but not hardy enough to withstand severe winter climates unless protected.

Trailing Roses Trailing roses are climbers adapted to planting on banks or walls. They produce long canes that creep along the ground, making a pleasing ground cover. Their flowers are not as attractive as other types, but they are hardy and have a place in some gardens.

Tree roses flanking a gate.

Tree, or Standard, Roses

Tree, or standard, roses are distinctive because of the form of the plant rather than the type of flower. They are made by grafting any of the bush-type roses on upright trunks. Tree roses usually must be staked for support, but they require very little space due to their primarily vertical growth. Many of the better-known varieties of bush roses are available as tree roses. Tree roses are used in formal plantings or are used to accent a particular part of the garden. In sections where winters are severe the plants need special protection.

POPULAR ROSES

Hybrid Tea	
Peace	Portrait
Butterscotch	Appollo
Flaming	J.F.K.
Sunset	White Wings

Floribunda	
Fashion	Roman Holiday
Oberon	Frensham
Allgold	Little Darling

Old-Fashioned	
Cabbage	Lancaster
Moss	York

Climbing	
Blaze	Rose Thor
Don Juan	Gold Rush
Dream Girl	

Tree	
Peace	Tropicana
Touch of Venus	

Buying Plants

Buy your rose plants from reputable sources. Generally, local nurseries and garden centers are good sources of planting material. Retail stores—drug stores, supermarkets, and department stores—also are good sources if their stock has been kept dormant and has been protected from drying.

You can also get a good selection of high-quality plants from mail-order nurseries and nursery departments of mail-order houses. Reputable mail-order organizations will send you catalogs listing the plants that they sell. They will guarantee their plants to grow and bloom if given normal care.

For help in deciding which of the many varieties of roses to buy, get catalogs from several of the large nurseries or nursery departments of mail-order houses. The varieties listed in these catalogs generally are favorites with rose growers, and you are likely to be satisfied with any of them.

Planting

Roses grow best where they have full sunshine all day. They will grow satisfactorily, however, if they have at least 6 hours of sun a day.

If you must plant roses where they are shaded part of the day and you have a choice as to morning sun or afternoon sun, plant them where they have morning sun. If plants are shaded in the morning, their leaves remain wet with dew a few hours longer than if they were in morning sun. Moisture on the leaves is favorable for the development of several leaf diseases.

Planting Times The proper time to plant packaged roses depends on the severity of winter temperatures in the area, as follows:

- If winter temperatures do not go below 10° Fahrenheit, plant at any time the bushes are fully dormant.
- If winter temperatures do not go below -10° Fahrenheit, plant in fall or spring.
- If winter temperatures regularly go below -10° Fahrenheit, plant in spring only.

Some nurseries and garden centers sell roses that are planted in containers. These container-grown roses can be transplanted at any time from spring to fall.

Spacing Plants When planting hybrid teas, grandifloras, polyanthas, and floribundas, space about 2 feet apart where winter temperatures are very cold (-10° Fahrenheit or below), about 2½ feet apart where winter temperatures are moderate (10° Fahrenheit to -10° Fahrenheit), and at least 3 feet apart where winter temperatures are mild (above 10° Fahrenheit). In all areas, space hybrid perpetuals 3 to 5 feet apart and climbers from 8 to 10 feet apart.

Soil Preparation If you are planting only a few roses, dig individual planting holes for them. Make the holes 12 inches deep and at least 18 inches in diameter. If you are planting a large number of roses in one bed, prepare the bed by spading the soil to a depth of about 12 inches. Then, dig planting holes in the prepared bed.

Any good garden soil will produce good roses. If you can grow good grass, shrubs, and other plants, your soil probably needs no special preparation for roses. If your soil is very heavy, or if it is light and lacking in fertility, or if the builder of your house has used subsoil from the basement excavation to level your lot, you can improve your soil by adding organic matter.

Use peat moss, leaf mold, or manure for organic matter. Most gardeners prefer to use manure. Dehydrated cow manure is available from garden-supply stores. If you use manure, add about one-half pound of superphosphate to each bushel. Spread a layer of organic matter 2 to 4 inches deep over the spaded bed. Work the organic matter into the soil to spade depth. If you are digging planting holes in unprepared soil, mix soil from the holes with organic matter. Use one part of peat or leaf mold to four parts of soil or one part of manure to six parts of soil. Mix thoroughly.

After planting holes are dug, either in beds or unprepared soil, loosen the soil in the bottom of the hole and work in about half a spadeful of well-rotted manure. Do not use fresh manure; it may injure any roots coming in contact with it.

Prepare beds and dig planting holes well in advance of planting so the plants can be set out as soon as they are received. Prepare the soil in fall, whether for fall or spring planting. If the soil has to be completely reworked, do it at least four weeks before planting.

Handling Plants Unless plants are frozen when they are delivered, unpack them at once. If they are frozen, store them where they can thaw out gradually; do not unpack them until they are completely thawed.

Inspect the roots for drying. If they are dry, soak them in warm (100° Fahrenheit) water for an hour or two.

The plants are best planted as soon as they are received. If you cannot plant them immediately, moisten the packing material and repack the plants. They can be kept this way safely for two to three days. If you must hold the plants for more than two or three days before planting, place them in a trench and cover the roots with moist soil. If the canes are dry, cover them with soil also.

When you are ready to set out the plants, examine their roots. Cut off all dead or injured growth. Remove broken or dead canes and, if necessary, cut the canes back to about 12 inches in length. Nurseries usually cut the tops back to about 12 inches before shipping the plants. If the tops have been cut back, do not cut them further; flowering usually is delayed if canes are cut back to less than 10 inches.

Protect the roots from drying at all times. Never expose them to sun or drying winds. Move the plants to the garden with their roots in a bucket of water or coat the roots with a thin clay mud and keep them covered with wet burlap or some other protection until planted.

Setting the Plants Place a small, cone-shaped pile of soil in the center of each planting hole. If winter temperatures in your area regularly go below -10° Fahrenheit, make the top of the cone low enough so the bud union of the plant is about 2 inches below the ground level. If the temperatures go below 10° Fahrenheit but not lower than -10° Fahrenheit, set the bud union 1 inch below ground level. If winter temperatures are warmer than 10°

Fahrenheit, set the bud union at the ground level or slightly below it.

Set the plant on the peak of the cone and spread the roots down the slope. Carefully work soil about the roots so all roots are in contact with the soil. When the roots are covered, add water to help settle the soil about the roots. Then fill the hole.

Mound the soil 8 to 10 inches high around the canes of bush and climbing roses and 3 to 4 inches high around the canes of miniature roses. Remove the soil mound when frost danger is past.

After setting tree roses, drive a sturdy pole into the soil beside the upright trunk and tie the trunk to the pole. This prevents the trunk from whipping in the wind and loosening the roots.

Cultivating and Mulching Cultivate roses carefully; their roots may grow close to the surface and may be injured by deep cultivation. The main purpose of cultivation is to remove weeds. This can be done by hand pulling the weeds or cutting them at the soil surface.

Use a mulch to aid in controlling weeds, conserving moisture, and adding fertility. Peat, ground corncobs, ground tobacco stems, buckwheat and cottonseed hulls, spent mushroom manure, and well-rotted strawy manure are effective as mulching materials.

Apply mulches about a month before the roses bloom. Remove all weeds and rake the soil lightly before applying mulches. Then spread the mulching material evenly around the plants to a depth of 2 or 3 inches. Keep the mulch on the soil throughout the year. The mulching material decays and becomes incorporated in the soil. Add new material as the mulch settles and becomes thin about the plants.

Watering Roses need large amounts of water. Even where rainfall is plentiful, occasional waterings are beneficial. Roses should receive the equivalent of 1 inch of water every seven to ten days throughout the growing season. Soak the soil thoroughly to a depth of 8 to 10 inches. Direct a small, slow-moving stream of water from a garden hose around the bases of the plants. A heavy stream usually is wasteful; most of the water runs off and fails to penetrate the soil more than a few inches.

Fertilizing

Roses grow best in soil that is medium to slightly acid (pH 5.5 to 6.5). To determine whether the acidity of your soil is within the best range for roses, have it tested or test it yourself. You can make your own test for soil acidity with testing kits sold by garden-supply stores. These kits are inexpensive and easy to use.

If you find the soil pH to be below 5.5, apply agricultural lime at a rate of 3 or 4 pounds per 100 square feet. If the pH is over 6.5, apply sulfur. Use 1 pound of sulfur per 100 square feet if the pH is between 7 and 7.5, 2 pounds if it is 8, and 3 pounds if it is 8.5. Wet soil; mix thoroughly. Allow to stand at least seven days before planting the bushes.

Acidity of the soil can change quickly; therefore, check the pH at monthly intervals after treating to see if another application of lime or sulfur is needed.

The fertilizer elements most likely to be deficient in garden soil are nitrogen, phosphorus, and potassium. To supply these elements, use a complete fertilizer. Grades 5-10-5, 4-8-4, or 4-8-6 are satisfactory.

Apply complete fertilizers at a rate of about 3 pounds per 100 square feet or 1 heaping tablespoon for each plant. Spread the fertilizer evenly around the plants, scratch it into the surface, and water.

Apply the fertilizer when new spring growth is well established and all danger of severe freezing is past. A second application can be made later in the season if the plants show evidence of mineral deficiencies—yellowing of leaves from lack of nitrogen, leaves turning grayish green from lack of phosphorus, or browning of leaf margins from lack of potassium. Do not apply fertilizers after July 15 in cold climates or after August 15 in mild climates. When applied late in the season, fertilizers may stimulate fresh growth and delay hardening of the wood before winter sets in.

Some soils are deficient in calcium. Calcium deficiency causes the margin of the rose leaflets to die. Eventually the entire leaf dies and drops off. The flowers may be deformed with brown spots near the margins of the petals. When these symptoms appear, run a soil test. If the pH value is below 5, add lime to build up the calcium supply.

Most soils are well supplied with iron, but in some sections of the country this deficiency causes the foliage to turn yellowish white. To correct it, spray the foliage with ferrous sulfate mixed at the rate of 1 ounce to 2 gallons of water, or spray with iron chelates, mixed according to directions on the package. Also run a test for pH. If the pH is above 7, add sulfur to lower it.

Pruning

Prune roses annually to improve their appearance, to remove dead wood, and to control the quantity and quality of flowers produced by the plants. If roses are not pruned, they soon grow into a bramble patch, and the flowers are small and of poor quality. Sometimes undesired shoots come from the understock. These should be removed as soon as they appear, or they are liable to dominate the plant.

Rose pruning is not difficult. Use sharp tools. A fine-toothed saw is useful for cutting dead canes. All other pruning can be performed with pruning

Properly pruned rosebushes develop beautiful, healthy, and fragrant flowers.

shears.

Do not leave bare stubs when pruning. Limit the cuts either to a cane, to the point on the crown from which the pruned member originated, or to a strong outward-facing bud.

Bush and Tree Roses Prune bush roses in early spring, just before growth starts. First remove the dead wood; be careful to cut an inch or so below the dark-colored areas. If no live buds are left remove the entire branch or cane.

Next, cut out all weak growth and any canes or branches growing toward the center of the bush. If two branches cross, remove the weaker.

Finally, shape the plant by cutting the strong canes to a uniform height. In mild climates, strong plants can be pruned to a height of 24 to 30 inches.

In some areas, the winters are so severe that much of the top of the plant is killed. Under these condi-tions, it is not possible to do much toward shaping the plants. Just cut out the dead wood, saving all the live wood you can.

Tree roses require heavy pruning in spring and some pruning during the growing season to keep the tops from becoming too large for the stem. After removing the dead wood, cut back the live canes to a length of 8 to 12 inches and shape the overall struc-ture of the plant.

Most of the shrub roses should be pruned after they have bloomed. As a rule, these plants are very hardy, so pruning is needed primarily to thin out and remove old canes. They do not require shaping; in almost all instances shrub roses are most attrac-tive when they are allowed to develop their natural shape.

Climbing Roses Prune hardy ramblers just af-ter they have flowered. This pruning stimulates new cane growth and development of new laterals on which the next year's flowers will be borne.

When ramblers are trained to a trellis or support so high that one season's growth will not cover it, cut off some of the older shoots. Shorten strong, vigorous canes. This pruning will stimulate laterals to develop and continue to elongate and eventually cover the trellis.

In spring remove all dead canes and weak branches. Prune sparingly; removal of too much wood at this time will reduce production of flowers.

Many of the large-flowered climbers—especially the everblooming types—do not produce as much growth each year as the hardier climbers. For this reason pruning must be less severe.

Cutting Flowers

Cutting rose flowers is an important cultural operation. Improper cutting can injure the plant and decrease its vigor. Use sharp tools to cut flowers. Breaking or twisting off flowers injures the remaining wood.

Do not cut any flowers during the first season of bloom. If early flowers are not cut, the plants usually develop into large bushes by fall. Some flowers may be cut then.

If you do not cut the flowers, remove them when their petals fall. Cut them with sharp shears or knife just above the topmost leaf. A withered individual flower in a cluster should be removed to give the remaining flowers more room to develop. After all flowers of a cluster have withered, cut off the entire stem just above the top leaf. This insures that the new side shoots will begin to develop.

Roses that are cut just before the petals start to unfold will continue to open normally and will remain in good condition longer than if they are cut after they are fully open. Roses will keep best if they are cut in late afternoon.

Winter Protection

Roses must be protected not only against low winter temperatures but also against fluctuating temperatures. Occasionally, rose varieties that are hardy in the North where winter temperatures are constantly low are injured during the winter in areas farther south where the temperature fluctuates considerably.

As the first step in avoiding winter injury, keep your roses healthy during the growing season. Roses that have been sprayed to control diseases and have been properly nourished are more likely to escape winter injury than plants that have lost their leaves because of diseases or nutrient deficiencies.

Bush Roses Immediately after the first killing frost, while the soil can still be easily worked, pile soil 8 to 10 inches high around the canes. It is best to bring in soil from another part of the garden for this; if you dig it from the rose beds you may injure the roots. After mounding soil about the canes, tie all the canes together to keep them from being blown about and loosening the root system. Inspect the plants frequently to be sure the soil is not washed away before the ground freezes. Protection by mounding usually is effective if the temperature does not drop below zero.

Where the temperature regularly goes below zero, further protection is necessary. Pile hay, straw, or strawy manure over the mounded canes. Hold it in place by throwing on a few shovelfuls of soil.

Remove covering materials—straw and soil—in spring as soon as danger of severe frost has passed. Remove the soil mound carefully to avoid breaking off any shoots that may have started to grow beneath the mound.

Tree Roses In areas where the temperature does not often go below zero, wrap the heads of the plants in straw and cover with burlap.

Where the temperature goes below zero, protect tree roses by covering the plants with soil. Do this by digging carefully under the roots on one side of the plants until the plants can be pulled over on the ground without breaking all root connections with the soil. Cover the entire plant with several inches of soil.

In spring, after the soil thaws and danger of severe frost is past, remove the soil cover and set the plants upright again.

Climbing Roses Climbing roses need protection in areas where the temperature regularly drops below zero. Lay the canes on the ground, hold them down with wire pins or notched stakes, and cover them with several inches of soil. Remove the soil in spring after danger of severe frost is past.

Propagation

Most varieties of roses can be propagated from cuttings taken during the summer or in fall.

Take summer cuttings after the flowers have fallen. Make 6- to 8-inch cuttings from the stems. Remove all leaves except one or two at the top. Plant the cuttings with half their length below the ground. Water them, then invert a fruit jar over them. Remove the fruit jar the following spring.

Take fall cuttings after the wood has ripened well. Cut the stems into 8- or 10-inch lengths, remove all leaves, and plant the cuttings in a well-protected sunny place with only the top bud above the ground. When freezing weather approaches, cover cuttings with a mulch of litter several inches deep to keep the ground from freezing.

Flowers

Flowers can be used in landscaping in much the same way as shrubs: as border plantings or as accents for trees or lawn areas. In a border planting, plant low-growing flowers in front, intermediate ones next, and tall plants in back. This prevents the taller plants from shading the small ones. Around foundations use flowers in front of taller shrubs and plants. Plant lawn or tree accents as you would a border planting, with smaller flowers on the outside and large plants in the center.

Flowers can be used in landscaping in much the same way as shrubs; as border plantings or as accents for trees or lawn areas. In a border planting, plant low-growing flowers in front, intermediate ones next, and tall plants in back. This prevents the taller plants from shading the small ones. Around foundations use flowers in front of taller shrubs and plants. Plant lawn or tree accents as you would a border planting, with smaller flowers on the outside and large plants in the center.

When planning flower areas in your landscape design consider these factors:

- the height and width of the full-grown plants
- the months or seasons you want the most color
- the colors you want in a specific planting area
- the sun exposure

Flowering Perennials

Perennials are flowering or foliage plants whose roots live from year to year. Their tops may or may not die back in the winter.

Some perennials flower the first year and can be grown as annuals to eliminate the problem of protecting them in the winter.

Perennials usually will not flower unless they develop to a certain size and are then exposed to low temperature for a number of weeks, then exposed to increasing day lengths and higher temperatures. Their flowering time is the result of this sequence of day length and temperature. Although perennials require constant care, they do well in most climates of the United States.

Among the most popular of the garden perennials are delphinium, alyssum, hollyhock, columbine, candytuft, carnation, and primrose.

Buying Plants or Seed You can buy many perennial plants from your local nursery or garden shop. These plants usually are in bloom when they are offered for sale, which allows you to select the colors you want for your garden. Buy perennial plants that are compact and dark green. Plants held in warm shopping areas are seldom vigorous. You can detect plants held in warm areas too long by the thin pale yellow stems and leaves. Do not buy these plants.

Named varieties are most useful in the garden— useful because we know their disease resistance, their heat and cold resistance, and their plant habits (height and branching). They are the backbone of a good perennial garden. Named varieties are available everywhere in the United States. Select plants of named varieties for special colors or growing habits. Propagate these by cuttings or clump divisions. Colors are definite from cuttings or divisions.

You can sow perennial seeds directly in the beds where the plants are to bloom. Many perennials are best grown from seed each year. Many of the so-called biennials (plants that flower the second year) are grown only from seed: columbine, foxglove, canterbury bells, and delphinium.

To get a good start toward raising vigorous plants, buy good seed. Be sure your seed is fresh. Do not buy it too far in advance of planting time; for best results, allow no more than a three-month interval. Old seed saved from previous years may lose much of its vitality under household conditions. It tends to germinate slowly and to produce poor seedlings.

Keep the seed dry and cool until you plant it. Special instructions for storage are printed on some seed packets. Follow these instructions.

Do not be in a rush to start seeds or to set out started plants. As a general rule, delay sowing seed outdoors or setting out plants until after the last frost. Most seeds will not germinate well until the soil warms to about 60°. If they are sowed in soil that is cooler than this, they will remain dormant until the soil warms and can rot before they germinate.

Start seed indoors no sooner than eight weeks before the average date for the last killing frost in your area. If you start seed earlier than this, the plants will be too large for satisfactory transplanting by the time the weather is warm enough for them to be set outside.

Selecting Perennials Select perennials for your particular area considering the factors listed earlier. Notice what grows well in local gardens, consult nurserymen, check with your state experiment station, and choose varieties that are most attractive to you.

Perhaps you have a specific purpose in mind; you can plant perennials as flowering edging plants, as accents in an evergreen planting, as flower masses by covering a single area with one species, as rock garden specimens, or as a screen of color. With a specific purpose, you can choose perennials for your garden by considering their characteristics and deciding which of the flowers meet your requirements.

Observe the flowering times of perennials in your area. That way you will be able to choose plants that will flower when nothing else is in bloom. The flowering time may vary by as much as six weeks from year to year, but plants of the same kind usually flower at the same time.

The list of plants given does not include all perennials. It is a selection of the more commonly used ones. These are the perennials that support and fill out a garden. You can obtain details on particular plants from plant societies and specialty books.

The following suggestions will enable you to grow perennials successfully:

- Prepare soil in the flower beds thoroughly.
- Start with vigorous plants or seeds. The best plan is to buy started plants or sow fresh seed where the plants are to grow. The least satisfactory plan is to start your own plants indoors.

FLOWERING PERENNIALS

Name	Height (Inches)	Blooming Season	Description	1	2	3	4	5	6	7	8	9	10
Achillea	8-24	Summer	good border plant, cut flowers			X	X	X	X	X	X		
Alyssum	9-12	Spring	good in dry, sandy soil					X	X	X	X	X	
Anemone	8-12	Spring	grown in rock gardens, cut flowers						X	X	X	X	X
Arabis	6-18	Spring	grows best in light shade			X	X	X	X	X	X		
Artemisia	12-30	Summer	grows in poor and dry soils						X	X	X		
Aster	18-50	Fall	does best in sunny bed				X	X	X	X	X	X	
Baby's Breath	30-45	Summer	source of cut flowers, good for drying			X	X	X	X	X	X	X	X
Begonia	8-12	Summer	good for shady, moist areas					X	X	X	X		
Candytuft	6-12	Spring	can be used as ground cover						X	X	X	X	
Canterbury Bells	12-30	Summer	use in borders, cut flowers					X	X	X	X		
Carnation	12-18	Summer	many landscape uses						X	X	X	X	X
Chrysanthemum	8-30	Fall	very popular in many uses		X	X	X	X	X	X			
Chinese Lanterns	12-24	Summer	produces bright orange seedpods					X	X	X	X	X	
Columbine	12-24	Spring	popular cut flower, needs rich soil					X	X	X	X	X	X
Coreopsis	18-30	All season	requires light loam, drought resistant				X	X	X	X	X	X	X
Daisy	6-24	Summer	hardy, adapts to most soils		X	X	X	X	X	X	X		
Day Lily	12-60	Summer	many species, used in borders					X	X	X	X	X	
Delphinium	24-48	All season	best for borders and background				X	X	X	X	X	X	
Dianthus	8-12	Spring	seeds germinate fast					X	X	X	X	X	X
Dicentra	10-18	Summer	good potted plant				X	X	X	X	X		
Foxglove	30-50	Summer	good for borders and cut flowers					X	X	X	X	X	X
Gaillardia	12-24	Summer	needs sun, can be very late bloomer				X	X	X	X	X		
Helleborus	10-15	Spring	used for borders and specimen plants					X	X	X	X	X	
Hibiscus	24-48	Summer	used in flower beds, cut flowers						X	X	X	X	X
Hollyhock	48-72	Spring	excellent background screen					X	X	X	X		
Hosta	12-18	All season	good foundation or ground cover					X	X	X	X	X	
Iris	12-40	Summer	popular cut flower, use in borders				X	X	X	X	X		
Liatris	24-48	Summer	easily started from seed		X	X	X	X	X	X	X		
Lily of the Valley	5-10	Spring	very popular edging and accent plant					X	X	X	X	X	X
Lupine	30-48	Spring	requires very good drainage					X	X	X	X	X	
Peony	18-36	Spring	hard to grow from seed		X	X	X	X	X	X			
Moss Phlox	4-6	Spring	drought resistant, needs sun					X	X	X	X	X	
Summer Phlox	12-24	Summer	borders or cut flowers					X	X	X	X	X	
Poppy	6-30	Spring	does not transplant well, needs sun				X	X	X	X	X	X	X
Primrose	4-6	Summer	easy to grow from seed						X	X	X		
Salvia	30-48	Summer	needs sun, good in borders					X	X	X	X	X	X
Sea Lavender	24-30	Summer	excellent for cutting and drying						X	X	X	X	X
Sunflower	72-90	Summer	produces edible seeds				X	X	X	X	X		
Sweet Pea	30-54	Fall	grows well on trellis or support				X	X	X	X	X	X	X
Tritoma	48-72	Summer	use in borders, cut flowers						X	X	X	X	
Trollius	12-30	Summer	requires extra moisture					X	X	X	X	X	
Veronica	6-30	Fall	very easy to grow, cut flowers					X	X	X	X	X	X
Violet	4-6	All season	good for any low landscaping use				X	X	X	X	X		

- Set out plants or sow seed at the recommended times. Plants set out too early may be killed by frost. Seeds will not germinate until the soil warms and, if sown too early, they may rot. However, early spring growth is important for the survival of many perennials.
- Provide the recommended distances between plants when thinning seedlings or setting out started plants. Proper spacing is necessary for full and proper plant development.
- Do not allow annuals to grow wildly in the same bed with perennials; they will crowd the perennials.
- Let the perennials stand out. Give them a background to show them off. Evergreens or wooden fences make excellent backgrounds.

Perennial flowers are very popular in gardens. Favorites include: (A) poppy, (B) rudbeckia, (C) dicentra, (D) columbine, (E) primrose, (F) gaillardia, (G) hollyhock, (H) aster, (I) phlox, (J) Canterbury bells, (K) daisy, (L) foxglove, (M) carnation, (N) hibiscus, (O) lupine.

- Do not consider perennials as permanent plants. Preparing the soil, replanting, and dividing old plants are essential for vigorous, flowering plants.

Preparing the Soil Preparing the soil is extremely important to perennials. Annuals can grow and flower in poorly prepared soil, but perennials seldom survive more than one year if the soil is not properly prepared.

Properly prepared soil should have:

- good drainage;
- protection from drying winds;
- adequate water in the summer.

If you prepare beds carefully, by spading deeply, providing adequate drainage, and lightening heavy soil with sand and organic matter, the flowers grown there are almost certain to be outstanding. Water enters well-prepared soil easily. Seed germinates readily; the plants grow deep, healthy roots, strong stems, and large, abundant flowers. The ben-

efits of careful soil preparation carry over from season to season. It is better to grow a small bed of flowers in well-prepared soil than to attempt to grow great masses of flowers in poorly prepared soil.

For new beds, begin preparing the soil in the fall before planting time. Before preparing new beds, test the soil to see that it is capable of absorbing water from rainfall. The soil must have water-holding capacity so that the plants will never be under stress. Dig a hole about 10 inches deep and fill with water. The next day, fill the hole with water again. If the water drains away in eight to ten hours, the permeability of the soil is sufficient for good growth.

If an appreciable amount of water remains in the hole after ten hours, it will be necessary to improve the drainage of the planting site or the soil will prevent proper development of roots. To improve drainage, bed up the soil. Dig furrows along the sides of the bed and add the additional soil to the bed to raise the level of the bed above the general level of the soil. Excess water can seep from the bed into the furrows. Water beds frequently during the summer because beds dry out faster than level soil.

After forming the beds, spade the soil to a depth of 8 to 10 inches. Remove large stones and any trash, but turn under all leaves, grass, stems, roots, and anything else that will decay easily. Respade three or four times at weekly intervals. If the soil dries between spadings, water it. Pull weeds before they set seed.

In spring, just before planting, spade again. At this spading, work peat moss, sand, fertilizer, and lime into the soil. For ordinary garden soil, use a 1-to 2-inch layer of peat moss and a 1-inch layer of unwashed sand, available from most building-supply yards. If your soil is heavy clay, double the amounts. By adding peat and sand to the soil each time you reset the plants, you can eventually improve even your subsoil to make a good garden soil. You could use well-rotted compost instead of peat moss.

Add a complete fertilizer such as 5-10-5 at the last spading. Use at a rate of 1½ pounds (3 rounded cups) per 100 square feet. Add ground limestone at a rate of 5 pounds (7 rounded cups) per 100 square feet.

Rake the soil surface smooth. After raking, the soil is ready for seeding or planting with started plants.

Add organic matter, either peat moss or compost, to the beds each year.

Setting Plants Whether you buy plants from a nursery or start your own indoors, set them out the same way. When the time comes to set plants out in the garden, remove them from flats by slicing downward in the soil between the plants. Lift out each plant with a block of soil surrounding its roots and set the soil block in a planting hole.

If the plants are in fiber pots, remove the paper from the outside of the root mass and set the plant in a prepared planting hole. When setting out plants in peat pots, remove the top edge of the pot to keep rain from collecting around the plant. Thoroughly moisten the pot and its contents to help the roots develop properly.

Drench the soil around the planting hole with a liquid fertilizer (16-52-10 or 20-20-20), mixed 1 tablespoon per gallon of water, to stimulate root growth.

Set the moistened pot in the planting hole and press the soil up around it. The pot will break down in the soil and improve the soil around the plant.

Allow plenty of space between plants because perennials need room to develop. Perennials usually show up best when planted in clumps or groups of plants of the same variety.

Planting Seed Outdoors Perennials seeded in the garden frequently fail to germinate properly because the surface of the soil cakes and prevents entry of water. To avoid this, sow the seed in vermiculite-filled furrows. Make the furrows in the soil about ½ inch deep. After filling them with fine vermiculite, sprinkle with water. Then make another shallow furrow in the vermiculite and sow the seed in this furrow. Sow it at the rate recommended on the packet. Cover the seed with a layer of vermiculite and, using a nozzle adjusted for a fine mist, water the seeded area thoroughly.

To retard water evaporation, cover the seeded area with sheets of newspaper or polyethylene film. Support the newspaper or plastic on blocks or sticks 1 or 2 inches above the surface of the bed. Remove the paper or plastic when seedlings appear.

When most outdoor-grown perennials develop two true leaves, they should be thinned to the recommended spacing. This allows the plants to have enough light, water, nutrients, and space for them to develop fully. If they have been seeded in vermiculite-filled furrows, the excess seedlings can be transplanted to another spot without injury.

Watering Do not rely on summer rainfall to keep your flower beds watered. Plan to irrigate them at regular intervals throughout the growing season. Allow water to penetrate deeply into the soil. Never water by hand—it requires too much time to do a thorough job, and it always tears up the soil structure and washes the beds.

When you water, moisten the entire bed thoroughly, but do not water so heavily that the soil becomes soggy. Water again when the soil is dry to touch and the tips of the plants wilt slightly at midday.

A canvas soaker hose is excellent for watering beds, but it is difficult to maintain because the canvas rots quickly. Water from the soaker hose seeps directly into the soil without waste. The slow-moving water does not disturb the soil or reduce its capacity to absorb water.

If you water with a sprinkler, use an oscillating sprinkler. This type covers a large area and produces rainlike drops of water. Do not use a rotating sprinkler; it tends to tear up the surface of the soil and covers only a small area.

The least effective method for watering is with a hand-held nozzle. Watering with a nozzle has all the objections of watering with a rotating sprinkler. In addition, gardeners seldom are patient enough to do a thorough job of watering with a nozzle, not enough water is applied, and the water that is applied usually is poorly distributed over the bed.

It is difficult to water plants in bloom. The flowers tend to rot if they catch and hold water.

If possible water in the early part of the day; this will allow plenty of time for the flowers and foliage to dry before night. Night watering increases the chances of disease.

Mulching Mulch gives an orderly look to the garden, cuts down weeds and weeding labor, and adds organic matter to the soil.

Trim the plants of excess foliage and stems before mulching. Mulch with buckwheat hulls, peat moss, salt hay, pine bark, pine needles, or wood chips. Select an organic material that will decompose slowly, that will allow water to penetrate to the soil below, and that adds a neutral color to the soil. Spread mulch 2 inches deep over the whole bed. Spread before the plants have made a great deal of growth. Water the mulch into place. All mulches require care to keep them attractive.

Mulch during both summer and winter.

Mulch during the summer to:

• retard water loss,
• prevent soil baking and cracking,
• hold down weeds,
• prevent soil splashing when watering.

Mulch during the winter to:

• protect newly planted perennials,
• protect less hardy plants.

Be careful with winter mulching; it can do more harm than good. Apply mulch around the plants only after the soil temperature has gone down, usually in the late fall after several killing frosts. If the winter mulch is applied too early, the warmth from the soil will cause new growth to start. Severe damage to the plant can result from new growth being frozen back. The best winter mulch is snow if the bed has good drainage.

A thin layer of peat moss is sufficient for a winter mulch. Keep winter mulch loose. It must be well drained and have good air circulation to keep the plants from rotting. Screen winter-mulched plants from the wind.

Remove the winter mulch as soon as growth starts in the spring. If you don't, the new growth will develop abnormally and have long, gangly stems and insufficient chlorophyll.

In many of the colder areas of the United States, spring planting of cold-frame-held plants is the only way to have a particular perennial in the garden.

Fertilizing Regularly fertilize the planting bed. Extensive growing time, required for perennials, robs the soil of its natural fertility.

Do not fertilize perennials heavily with inorganic fertilizers. A light fertilization program gives a continuous supply of nutrients to produce plants that are easier to train or support on stakes and plants that do not have dense foliage which interferes with air circulation.

Put little rings of 5-10-5 fertilizer around each plant in early spring (March). Repeat about six weeks later, and again six weeks after that. This should be enough to carry plants through the summer. Apply another treatment of fertilizer to late-blooming plants in late summer or early fall.

Always water the bed after applying fertilizer to wash the fertilizer off the foliage and prevent fertilizer burn. It will also make the fertilizer available to the plant immediately. Until the fertilizer enters the soil, regardless of how long it has been on the surface of the soil, it is not available to the plant.

Cultivating After plants are set out or are thinned, cultivate only to break crusts on the surface of the soil. When the plants begin to grow, stop cultivating. Pull weeds by hand frequently in limited areas. As plants grow, feeder roots spread out between them; cultivation is likely to injure these roots. In addition, cultivation stirs the soil and uncovers other weed seeds that then germinate.

Staking Many perennials are top-heavy and need staking.

If plants fall over, the stem will function poorly. If the stem is cracked, rot organisms can penetrate the break.

Stake plants when you first set them out so they will grow to cover the stakes, will be turned to face the front of the bed, and will better withstand driving rain and wind.

You can use stakes made of twigs, wood dowels, bamboo, wire, or even plastic. Select stakes that will be 6 to 12 inches shorter than the height of the grown plant.

Place the stakes behind the plants. Sink the stakes into the ground far enough to be firm. Loosely tie plants to the stakes. Use wire covered with a layer of paper or plastic to tie the plants. Do not use string; string rots and is unsightly. Tie the plant, making a double loop of the wire with one loop around the plant and the other around the stake. Never loop the wire around both stake and plant; the plant will hang to one side, and the wire may girdle the stem.

Dividing Never leave a perennial planted in the same place for more than three years. The center of the clump will grow poorly, and the flowers will be sparse. The clump will deplete the fertility of the soil in which it is grown.

Divide mature clumps of perennials. Select only vigorous side shoots, the outer part of the clump which will grow best. Discard the center of the clump. Divide the plant into clumps of three to five shoots each. Be careful not to overdivide; too small a clump will not give much color the first year after replanting.

Divide perennials in the fall in southern areas and in the spring in northern areas.

Discard extra plants, give them to friends, or plant them elsewhere in your yard.

Making Cuttings Many plants can be propagated from either tip or root cuttings. Generally, tip cuttings are easier to propagate.

Make tip cuttings 3 to 6 inches long. Treat the base of the cutting with a root stimulant. Leave all foliage on the cutting except the part that will be below the soil line. Insert one cutting in each peat pot.

To make root cuttings dig the plants in late summer, after they have bloomed. Select pencil-size roots; cut them into 4-inch sections. Put each piece in a peat pot.

Prepare a tray of peat pots as for seeds, except the soil mix should be 2 parts sand, 1 part soil, and 1 part peat moss. Water thoroughly.

Place the tray of tip cuttings in a lightly shaded place. Cover with a sheet of plastic. Check regularly to make sure the cuttings do not dry out. When the cuttings do not pull easily out of the soil, they have begun to root. Make holes in the plastic sheet to let air in and to harden the cuttings. Every few days make new holes, or make the holes larger. Finally, remove the cover. Allow the cuttings to grow. Pinch back their tips ten days after the cover is removed to promote branching. Transplant the rooted cuttings to a freshly prepared bed in midsummer.

Flowering Annuals

Garden annuals are easy to grow and generally do well in all parts of the United States. Among the most popular of the garden annuals are zinnias, marigolds, petunias, and ageratums. You can sow annual seeds directly in the beds where the plants are to bloom, or you can start early plants indoors. You also can buy started plants of many annuals from your local nursery or garden shop. It is an easy task to prepare beds and set out these started plants. The plants provide color from the time they are set out until they are killed by fall frosts.

To grow annuals successfully follow these rules:
- Start with vigorous plants or seeds. Buy started plants or sow fresh seed where the plants are to grow.
- Prepare soil in the flower beds thoroughly.
- Set out plants or sow seed at the recommended times.
- Provide the recommended distances between plants when thinning seedlings or setting out started plants. Proper spacing is necessary for fullest development of the plants.

Selecting Annuals You probably already have decided which annuals you want to grow; annuals are high on everyone's list of favorite flowers.

Perhaps you have a specific purpose in mind for annuals: to provide a mass of color for brightening the dark foliage of background shrubs, to fill in beds until shrubs grow large enough to be decorative in their own right, or to overplant bulb beds to provide color after spring-flowering bulbs have bloomed. If so, you can choose annuals for your garden by considering their characteristics and deciding which of the flowers meet your requirements.

Some annuals are best for use as bedding plants, grouped to give large masses of color in the garden. Some are best as border plants. Some are best for low edging around beds and walks, and some tall varieties are best used as quick-growing screens. Whatever your requirements for garden flowers, you probably can find an annual flowering plant that is suitable.

Buying Seed To get a good start toward raising vigorous plants, buy good seed. Keep the seed dry and cool until you plant it. Follow the special instructions for storage printed on some seed packets.

Preparing the Soil Satisfactory results in growing annuals depend, to a large extent, on thorough preparation of the soil where the plants are to grow. You can make a scratch in the soil and plant seeds in the scratch, and you will probably have flowers growing there before the season is over. But the plants will be spindly and the flowers sparse.

On the other hand, if you prepare beds for annuals as carefully as you would for perennials (by spading deeply, providing adequate drainage, and lightening heavy soil with sand and organic matter) the flowers grown there are almost certain to thrive. Follow the soil preparation techniques given for perennials in a previous section of this chapter.

Planting Times Many annuals can be seeded throughout the growing season for a prolonged display of color. Proper times for seeding most of the

PLANTING AND CULTURE OF SELECTED GARDEN ANNUALS

Plant	Height (Inches)	Blooming Season	When to Plant Seed	Exposure	Germination Time (Days)	Plant Spacing (Inches)	Remarks
Ageratum	6-20	Summer	After last frost	Semishade or full sun	5	10 to 12	Pinch tips of plants to encourage branching. Remove dead flowers.
Baby's Breath	12-18	Summer	Early spring or in summer	Sun	10	10 to 12	Make successive sowings for prolonged blooming period. Shade summer plantings.
Balsam	20-28	Summer	After last frost	Sun	10	12 to 14	
Calendula	14-18	Summer	Early spring or late fall	Shade or sun	10	8 to 10	
Calliopsis	18-24	All season	After last frost	Shade or sun	8	10 to 14	
Candytuft	10-15	Spring	Early spring or late fall	Shade or sun	20	8 to 12	
Cockscomb	16-40	Summer	Early spring or late fall	Shade or sun	10	10 to 12	
Coleus	20-24	Spring	Sow indoors anytime; outdoors after last frost.	Sun or partial shade	10	10 to 12	
Cornflower	16-36	Summer	Early spring	Partial shade	5	12 to 14	
Cosmos	30-48	Fall	After last frost	Sun	5	10 to 12	
Dahlia	18-40	Spring	After last frost	Sun	5	12 to 14	For maximum bloom, sow several weeks before other annuals.
Forget-Me-Not	8-12	Summer	Spring or summer; shade in summer.	Partial shade	10	10 to 12	
Four-O'clock	20-24	Fall	After last frost	Sun	5	12 to 14	Store roots, plant next year.
Globe Amaranth	18-24	Summer	Early spring	Sun	15	10 to 12	
Impatiens	10-12	Spring	Indoors anytime. Set out after last frost.	Partial shade or deep shade.	15	10 to 12	
Larkspur	18-48	Spring	Late fall in South, early spring in North.	Sun	20	6 to 8	Difficult to transplant; grow in peat pots.
Lupine	18-24	Spring	Early spring or late fall	Sun	20	6 to 8	Soak seed before planting. Guard against damping-off.
Marigold	8-24	All season	After last frost	Sun	5	10 to 14	High fertility delays bloom.
Morning Glory	10-12	Summer	After last frost	Sun	5	24 to 36	Reseeds itself.
Nasturtium	8-12	All season	After last frost	Sun	8	8 to 12	For best flowers, grow in soil of low fertility.
Pansy	6-10	All season	Spring or summer; shade in summer.	Sun or shade	10	6 to 8	Does best in cool season.
Petunia	8-24	All season	Late fall (in South)	Sun	10	12 to 14	Start early in spring indoors. Keep cool.
Phlox	6-12	All season	Early spring	Sun	10	6 to 8	Make successive plantings for prolonged bloom.
Poppy	12-16	Summer	Early spring through summer; shade in summer.	Sun	10	6 to 10	Difficult to transplant; start in peat pots. Make successive plantings.
Rudbeckia	20-24	Summer	Spring or summer; shade in summer.	Sun or partial shade.	20	10 to 14	Perennial grown as annual. Blooms first year.
Salpiglossis	24-30	Spring	Early spring	Sun	15	10 to 12	Needs supports. Avoid cold, heavy soil.
Snapdragon	8-30	Summer	Spring or late fall	Sun	15	6 to 10	Start cool, pinch tips to encourage branching.
Spider Plant	30-40	Summer	Early spring; spring or fall.	Sun	10	12 to 14	Reseeds freely. Pinch to keep plant short. Water and fertilize freely.
Strawflower	30-40	Spring	Early spring	Sun	5	10 to 12	
Sunflower	60-80	Summer	After last frost	Sun	5	12 to 14	
Sweet Alyssum	6-8	Summer	Early spring	Sun	5	10 to 12	Damps off easily. Sow in hills; do not thin.
Sweet Pea	36-90	Spring	Early spring or late summer through late fall.	Sun	15	6 to 8	Select heat-resistant types.
Verbena	9-12	Summer	After last frost	Sun	20	18 to 24	Pinch tips often to encourage branching.
Vinca	15-18	Summer	After last frost	Sun	15	10 to 12	Avoid overwatering.
Zinnia	18-36	Summer	After last frost	Sun	5	8 to 12	Thin after plants begin to bloom; remove poor-flowering plants.

common annuals are listed on the seed packages.

Setting Started Plants and Sowing Seeds By setting started plants in your garden, you can have a display of flowers several weeks earlier than if you sow seeds of the plants. Use of started plants is especially helpful for annuals that are slow to germinate or that need several months to bloom. Examples of these slow-to-bloom annuals: candytuft, gaillardia, lupine, rudbeckia, and verbena.

You can buy plants of these and many other annuals, or you can start your own. Annual plants can be set or their seeds sown in the garden in the same manner as perennials.

Thinning When most outdoor-grown annuals develop two true leaves, they should be thinned to the recommended spacing.

Zinnias are an exception to this rule of thinning. In every variety of zinnias will appear plants with undesirable flowers of the "Mexican-hat" type. The

Popular garden annual flowers include: (A) baby's breath, (B) pansy, (C) marigold, (D) coleus, (E) snapdragon, (F) sunflower, (G) sweet pea, (H) calliopsis, (I) impatiens, (J) zinnia, (K) forget-me-not, (L) petunia, (M) morning glory, (N) ageratum, (O) dahlia.

only way to avoid having these undesirable flowers in your garden is to wait until the plants have bloomed for the first time before you thin them to their final spacing. The recommended spacing for zinnias is 8 to 12 inches. When the plants develop two true leaves, thin them to 4 to 6 inches, transplanting the extra plants. When they bloom (they will still be quite small) pull and destroy plants having the undesirable flowers. Thin the remaining plants to the 8- to 12-inch spacing.

Another exception to the rule for thinning is sweet alyssum. This annual is particularly susceptible to damping-off. To insure a good stand of plants, sow the seed in hills and do not thin the seedlings.

Watering Water flowering annuals as you would perennials. For proper mulching, fertilizing, cultivating, and cutting methods refer to the perennial section.

Drying Plants As for cut flowers, grow plants for drying in a section of the garden by themselves. Remove whole plants for drying at the following times:

Plant	Time to Cut
Baby's Breath	When flowers are well formed.
Cockscomb	When in color but before seed sheds.
Gaillardia	When in full color but before petals dry.
Globe Amaranth	When mature.
Larkspur	When oldest floret matures; plant forms a spike.
Strawflower	When buds begin to open.
Zinnia	When in full color but before petals begin to dry.

After cutting, hang the plants upside down in a shady place to dry. Use them in flower arrangements during the winter.

Starting Perennial and Annual Plants Indoors

Unless you are willing to invest in special lighting equipment and to devote considerable care to starting plants indoors, it usually is best to buy plants or to sow seed of annuals directly in the garden. Home-started plants seldom are as satisfactory for setting out as those bought from nurserymen. They seldom grow as well or bloom as prolifically as those planted directly in the garden.

Home-started seedlings frequently are attacked by a fungus disease, damping-off. Those seedlings that escape the disease usually are weak and spindling and never become good garden plants; conditions of light, temperature, and humidity normally found in the home are not favorable for plant growth.

Damping-Off Damping-off causes seeds to rot and seedlings to collapse and die. The disease is carried in soil and may be present on planting containers and tools. Soil moisture and temperature necessary for germination of seeds also are ideal for development of damping-off.

The disease can be prevented. Before planting treat the seed with a fungicide, sterilize the soil, and use sterile containers.

Treat the seed with thiram. Tear off the corner of the seed packet and, through the hole in the packet, insert about as much fungicide dust as you can pick up on the tip of the small blade of a penknife. Close the hole by folding over the corner of the packet, then shake the seed thoroughly to coat it with the fungicide dust.

Sterilize the soil in an oven. Fill a container with moist, but not wet, soil, bury a raw potato in the center of the soil, and bake the container of soil in a medium oven. When the potato is cooked, the soil should be sterile.

To avoid introducing the damping-off organism on containers, use fiber seed flats or peat pots. These containers are sterile, inexpensive, and readily available from garden shops. Fiber flats are light and strong. They are inexpensive and can be thrown away after one use. Peat pots can be set out in the garden along with the plants they contain; roots of the plants grow through the walls of the pots. Plants grown in peat pots suffer no setback when they are transplanted to the garden. Larkspur and poppy, which ordinarily do not tolerate transplanting, can be grown in peat pots satisfactorily.

If you use wooden boxes or clay flowerpots for soil containers, clean them well. Soak clay pots in water and scrub them well to remove all of the white fertilizer crust from the outside.

Sterilize clay pots and boxes by baking them in the oven when you are sterilizing the soil mixture, or swab the pots and boxes with a solution of one part chlorine bleach to ten parts water. Allow the containers to dry thoroughly before filling them with soil.

If, despite your precautions, damping-off appears in your seedlings, it is best to discard the containers and soil and start over.

Starting Seeds The best soil for starting seeds is loose, well drained, fine textured, and low in nutrients. To prepare a soil having these properties, mix equal parts of garden soil, sand, and sphagnum peat moss.

Fill soil containers about two-thirds full with this mixture. Level the soil and soak it thoroughly. Then sift more of the soil mixture through window screening to form a layer that fills one-fourth to one-half of the remaining depth of the container.

Make a furrow ¼ inch deep in the fine soil. Sow large-seeded plants—cosmos, zinnia, marigold, nasturtium, cornflower, sweet pea, morning glory, or four-o'clock—directly in the bottom of the furrow. Before sowing small-seeded plants, fill the furrow with vermiculite; sow small seeds on the surface of the vermiculite.

Sow seed in flats at the rate recommended on the seed packet. If you are growing large-seeded plants in peat pots, sow two to four seeds in each pot.

After you have sowed the seeds, cover all furrows with a thin layer of vermiculite, then water with a fine mist. Place a sheet of polyethylene plastic over the seeded containers and set them in the basement or some other location where they can be kept at a temperature between 60° and 75°.

The containers need no further water until after the seeds have germinated, and they need no light. Under no circumstances should the plastic-covered containers be placed in sunlight; heat buildup under the plastic could kill emerging seedlings.

Raising Seedlings As soon as the seed has germinated, remove the plastic sheeting and place the seedlings in the light. Many gardeners supply light to the seedlings by placing the containers on a windowsill. This practice usually is unsatisfactory.

For best results, seedlings should be raised under lighting conditions that can be closely controlled for intensity and duration. Use a fluorescent tube as the light source. For proper intensity, place the containers 6 inches below the tube. Control the duration of lighting by connecting the fluorescent fixture to a timer.

Some plants develop best for setting out if they are grown under short-day conditions—ten to twelve hours of light each day. Under these conditions they produce compact plants that flower only after they are set outside. These plants usually do best if the temperature is kept between 60° and 65°. Grow the following seedlings on short days:

Calliopsis	Poppy
Cornflower	Portulaca
Gaillardia	Rudbeckia
Globe Amaranth	Salpiglossis
Petunia	Snapdragon
Phlox	Verbena

Most plants need longer days—eighteen hours of light each day. If they are started on short days they soon begin to form flowers, and they never become good bedding plants. Grow the following seedlings with a day length of eighteen hours and a temperature of 65°:

Cockscomb	Morning Glory
Cosmos	Scarlet Sage
Dahlia	Sunflower
Marigold	Zinnia

If your plants are on neither of these lists, grow them with a day length of eighteen to twenty hours.

Day length is not important for plants grown at temperatures of 50° to 55°. However, seedlings grown at these low temperatures develop more slowly than those grown at 60°.

After the plastic is removed from the container, the new plants must be watered frequently, and they must be fertilized. You can do both of these jobs at one time by using a solution made by mixing 1 tablespoon of soluble fertilizer in 1 gallon of water.

When you use this solution, moisten the soil thoroughly. Be careful not to wash out the seedlings when you water them. To avoid this, use a rubber-bulb syringe, available from garden stores. If you do not have a syringe, you can place the solution in a container that is somewhat larger than the seed containers and submerge the pots or flats up to their rims in the solution. This waters the plants from the bottom. Remove the pots or flats from the solution as soon as the soil is thoroughly moistened.

You also can water flats without disturbing the soil if you sink a small flower pot in the center of the flat and pour the water in the pot.

Transplanting When seedlings develop two true leaves, thin those that are in peat pots to one seedling per pot. Transplant those in flats to other flats. Using a knife or spatula, dig deeply under the seedlings in the flats, lifting a group of the seedlings. Let the group of seedlings fall apart and pick out individual plants from the group. Handle the seedlings as little as necessary. Don't pinch them. Set the seedlings in new flats that contain the same soil mixture as was used for starting the seed. Space the seedlings about 1½ inches apart in the flats.

Water thoroughly and replace the seedlings under the fluorescent lights. Continue watering and fertilizing the plants until time for setting them out.

If you must hold seedlings indoors longer than eight weeks after sowing, transplant them to a flat containing pure sphagnum moss. Do not fertilize them. For best results, however, plan ahead so that it is unnecessary to hold seedlings longer than eight weeks.

Bulbs

Spring can be more than a release from hours spent indoors because of discouraging weather. It can be a fragrant, colorful experience as beautiful tulips, narcissus (daffodils and jonquils), hyacinths, and crocuses blossom forth. By selecting a variety of bulbs with different blooming times, you can create an array that will enhance your landscape from March, long before your other plants produce their buds, to August.

The true bulb is made up of layers of fleshy tissue encasing a storehouse of food that is released during the early stages of root development and growth. When the flower is in full bloom, this food is depleted; but it is uniquely replenished in time to sustain the bulb during its dormant season.

Selecting Bulbs Although bulbs did not originate with the Dutch, they are rightly credited with improving and perfecting them. The Dutch government will allow the export of only those bulbs that are large enough to produce a full-size flower, making Holland-grown bulbs the best value for the money. There is no such thing as a bargain when purchasing bulbs. Those sold at low prices may have been grown domestically, stored improperly, or damaged, and they may not produce full-size flowers the first year.

All varieties of bulbs will do well in temperate climates. Most will grow in warmer regions of the South, but hyacinths, paper-white narcissus, and daffodils (except the double and white varieties) do especially well. Although it is more difficult to grow tulips in some southern climates, many of the early bloomers have been successful.

It is generally agreed that for the best effect bulbs should be planted in groups of five to fifteen, depending on the amount of space available. When deciding how many to buy, you can estimate that an average group of ten bulbs will cover about 1½ to 2 square feet.

Select several different types of bulbs to achieve the variety of heights and colors you desire. If you are unsure of which bulbs to buy or the number you will require, take a sketch of your planting area to your nurseryman and ask him to assist you.

Be sure the bulbs are free of disease. Diseased bulbs look moldy, discolored, or soft and rotted. Bulbs should be firm with an unblemished skin.

Store bulbs in a cool, dry area. A temperature of 60 to 65°F is cool enough to prevent most bulbs from drying out until you plant them.

Planting Bulbs Most bulbs can be planted any time from September 1 to December 1 in temperate climates and from November 1 to February 1 in the South. In warmer southern regions, precooling the bulbs by storing them in a refrigerator for six to eight weeks before planting has been found to greatly improve their growth. Hyacinths, crocuses, and narcissus should be planted immediately after they are purchased.

You can start many bulbs in flats or pots indoors in winter or early spring and replant them outdoors when the danger of spring frost has passed. Specific planting times are given on the bulb package.

Most bulbs need full sunshine. Try to select a planting site that will provide at least six to ten hours of direct sunlight a day. Bulbs planted in a southern exposure near a building or wall bloom earlier than bulbs planted in a northern exposure.

Prepare flower beds and border areas that are well drained for your bulbs (most failures can be traced to improper soil drainage) by weeding and leveling with a rake. For best results in warm climates, select cool, shady areas that can be watered periodically to retain moisture. Check the soil requirements for the types of bulbs you are planting. Unless otherwise specified, fertilize with bone meal (5 pounds per 100 square feet) and pulverized sheep manure (10 pounds per 100 square feet), and spread a 1-inch layer of compost. Bone meal is an excellent source of nitrogen but releases the nitrogen slowly enough that the bulbs are not harmed. Most bulbs, if planted in well-prepared soil that is free of tree and shrub roots, will reappear for many seasons.

Dig and plant your flower beds when the soil is fairly dry. Wet soil packs tightly and retards plant growth. If you can crumble the soil between your fingers, it is dry enough for digging and planting. Spade the soil 8 to 12 inches deep. As you dig, remove all debris. All bulbs require low levels of fertilizer. Avoid frequent applications of high nitrogen fertilizers; this will promote rotting in the bulbs.

Before actually planting, arrange the bulbs on top of the soil to assure that they will be grouped by size and color in the design of your choice. Then place the bulbs in holes of the proper depth and spacing.

Plant bulbs upright, and press the soil firmly over them to prevent air pockets underneath. Water the planted beds thoroughly to help settle the bulbs in the soil.

In loose, sandy soil, plant bulbs 3 to 4 inches deeper than the depths recommended in the list of bulbs.

Be sure to plant bulbs at recommended distances apart because many of them need room to develop new offshoots.

Care of Plants If weeds grow in your flower beds, you can usually pull them by hand. Be careful when you use a hoe or other weeding tool; these implements may injure plant stems and surface roots.

Normal rainfall usually provides enough moisture for flowering bulbs, but during dry weather, you should water the plants at weekly intervals. When you water, soak the ground thoroughly.

Be sure to keep fertilizer off the leaves and away from bulbs and roots to avoid burning them.

When flowers fade, cut them off to prevent seed formation. Seeds take stored food from the bulbs.

After the leaves turn yellow, dig the bulbs and store them for replanting the next year. Destroy the dead stems and foliage of the plants. Foliage left on the ground may carry disease to new growth the next year. If disease is severe, plant bulbs in a new location.

Be sure also to follow the special instructions given for each plant. If the general instructions conflict with the special instructions, follow the special instructions.

Helpful Hints In cold climates, protect the bulbs with hay, straw, or peat moss during the winter months.

If you are bothered by rabbits, gophers, or other potential bulb-eaters, use a commercial repellent or mix a few crushed mothballs with the top inch of soil. Rodent repellent or poison set around the beds at planting time will deter mice that might travel through mole tunnels in search of tender bulbs.

Always rotate tulips each year to prevent "tulip fire," which will destroy the plant. If need be, substitute other bulbs such as the crocus, hyacinth, or narcissus which are not affected by this disease.

When cutting blossoms for indoor arrangements, do not take too much foliage or you may remove

GUIDE FOR SELECTING AND PLANTING BULBS

Bulb	Planting Time*	Depth and Spacing	Soil and Climate	Height (Inches)	Blooming Time	Color
Achimenes	after last frost	6″ deep, 3-4″ apart	well-drained, shade	8 to 12	early summer	various
Allium	early spring	2-3″ deep, 6-10″ apart	well-drained	9 to 48	June to July	white, red, yellow, blue, pink
Amaryllis	early May	just below surface, 12-18″ apart	well-fertilized, rich	12 to 36	June to July	white, red, pinks
Begonia	early spring	2-3″ deep, 8-12″ apart	light shade, cool	12 to 24	various	various
Caladium	early spring	6″ deep, 5-6″ apart	shade	9 to 18	June to August	pink, red, white
Calla Lily	fall	6″ deep, 8″ apart	rich, sun or partial shade	10 to 36	May to July	red, yellow, white, pink
Canna	spring	just below surface, 12-18″ apart	well-fertilized, sun	18 to 36	June to August	various
Crocus	Sept. 1 to Dec. 15	3″ deep, 3-4″ apart	well-drained, rich, sunny	4 to 6	March 15 to 30	white, purple, yellow
Dahlia	fall	3-4″ deep, 12-24″ apart	rich loam, full sun	10 to 80	summer, fall	various
Day Lily	early spring, late summer	just below surface, 18-24″ apart	well-fertilized	6 to 72	various	red, pink, orange, yellow
Gladiolus	early spring	4-7″ deep, 6-8″ apart	well-fertilized, sun	24 to 48	various	various
Hyacinth	Sept. 1 to Dec. 15	3″ deep, 4″ apart	well-fertilized, sandy	10 to 12	end of April	white, red, yellow, pinks, blues
Iris	fall	4-7″ deep, 8-10″ apart	well-drained	18 to 36	early spring	various
Lilies	fall or early spring (except *candidum*)	depth equal to twice the height of bulb, 6″ apart for smaller bulbs, 12″ apart for larger bulbs	well-drained, slightly acid (except *candidum*), partial shade	2 to 9	June to August	various
Montbretia	early spring	4-7″ deep, 6-8″ apart	well-drained, sun	24 to 36	August to September	orange, red, gold, yellow
Narcissus						
Daffodil (large cup)	Sept. 1 to Dec. 1	6″ deep, 3-6″ apart	deep loam enriched with organic fertilizer	15 to 16	April 15 to 30	yellow, white
Jonquil	Sept. 1 to Dec. 1	6″ deep, 5″ apart		16 to 18	April 20 to May 5	deep yellow
Trumpet Daffodil	Sept. 1 to Dec. 1	6″ deep, 5-6″ apart		18 to 20	April 10 to 25	yellow, yellow-orange, white, scarlet
Star-of-Bethlehem	early spring	4″ deep, 4-6″ apart	well-drained, partial shade	12 to 14	July to September	various
Tuberose	spring	2-3″ deep, 8-12″ apart	well-drained, sunny	12 to 24	September	white
Tulips (early)						
Single Double	Sept. 15 to Oct. 15 (before frost occurs)	5-6″ deep, 5″ apart	well-drained, shade in cold climate	10 to 15	April 15 to 30	various

Plant two months later in the South.

much of the bulb's food supply needed for next year's growth. The result could be poor blossoms or no blossoms at all.

Never dig up any of the bulbs for storage or transplanting until the flowers have faded and the bulb has ceased growing for the season.

Store bulbs at a temperature as close to the temperature of the soil where they have been planted. Never store lilies. If left out of the ground even for short periods of time, they will dry up and be of no use.

Most flowering bulbs should be dug and stored when the leaves on the plants turn yellow. Use a spading fork to lift the bulbs from the ground. Wash off any soil that clings to the bulbs, except for bulbs that are stored in pots or with the soil around them.

Leave the soil on achimenes, begonia, canna, caladium, dahlia, and ismene bulbs. Store these bulbs in clumps on a slightly moistened layer of peat moss or sawdust in a cool place. Wash and separate them just before planting.

Spread the washed bulbs in a shaded place to dry. When dry store them away from sunlight in a cool, dry basement, cellar, garage, or shed at 60 to 65°F. Avoid temperatures below 50° or above 70°F unless different instructions are given for a particular bulb.

Inspect your bulbs for signs of disease. Keep only large healthy bulbs that are firm and free of spots. Discard undersized bulbs. Separate your bulbs by species or variety before storing them.

Popular bulb flowers and plants include: (A) caladium, (B) iris, (C) peony, (D) tuberose, (E) gladiolus, (F) begonia, (G) calla, (H) dahlia, (I) allium.

Tulips are the most popular bulb.

If you have only a few bulbs, you can keep them in paper bags hung by strings from the ceiling or wall. Store large numbers of bulbs on trays with screen bottoms. Be sure that air can circulate around them. Never store bulbs more than two or three deep; deep piles of bulbs generate heat and cause decay.

Tubers and Corms Although bulbs, corms, and tubers are all referred to as bulbs, they differ in appearance.

A true bulb is composed of layers of flesh, or scales, that overlap each other like the layers of an onion. A complete flowering plant develops inside the bulb. Each year, the growing plant replaces the bulb either partially or entirely.

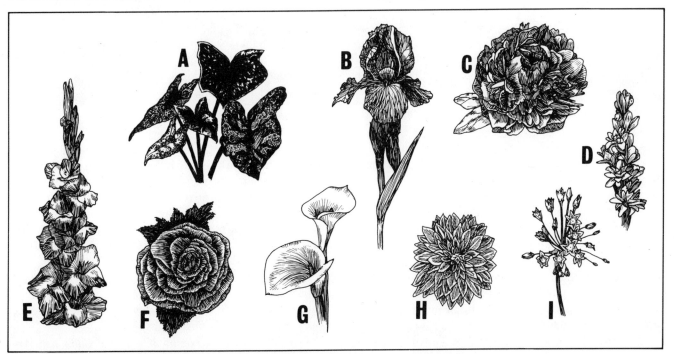

Hyacinths, tulips, daffodils, and crocus: four very popular spring-flowering bulbs.

A corm is a swollen underground stem that grows upright. Each year, the growing plant produces a new corm on top of the old one. The plant grows from the top of the corm.

A tuber is the swollen end of an underground side shoot that has eyes, or growing points. Each eye produces a separate plant.

Tubers multiply from year to year and may be cut apart, or divided, to increase the number of plants you can have in your garden. When tubers are divided for replanting, each division must have eyes on it. Tubers without eyes will not grow.

The most popular tuber is the begonia. Tuberous begonias can be started indoors in March by placing the bulbs about 3 inches apart in a flat and covering them with 1 inch of dirt. After four weeks, if there is no danger of frost, they can be removed and planted outdoors. The bulbs should be spaced about 1 foot apart and planted so that there is 2 to 3 inches of soil over the apex (top) of the plant. They will bloom in August.

After the first frost, remove the bulbs from the ground, permitting any loose dirt to remain on them. Store them in a cool, dry place until the next season, then clean and replant them.

The best known corms are the crocus and the

gladiolus. Glads will thrive in any type of soil. Bulbs should be spaced 3 to 5 inches apart and planted 4 inches deep. The unique feature of these bulbs is that after the frost is completely out of the ground, they can be planted in three-week intervals until the end of June for continuous blooming all season. For best results plant all gladiolus in sunlight and dust them every two weeks until flowers are in full bloom.

In the autumn, cut off any foliage as close to the apex as possible. Once the glads have been dug out of the ground, they can be stored in a cool, dark place until they are ready to be replanted the next season.

Indoor Bulbs You can enjoy the beauty of flowers the year round by growing bulbs indoors during the winter. Almost any bulb will do well, but crocuses, hyacinths, and certain varieties of daffodils and tulips are best suited for indoor growing. Three to four bulbs planted in each container will give a full-blossom effect.

All you will need is the bulbs, a container with a good drainage hole, soil, and a cool area with no direct sunlight. Just follow these simple steps:

1. Cover the pot's drainage hole with a few stones to prevent clogging and the loss of soil. For better drainage, place a fine layer of sand on the bottom of the pot.
2. Mix your potting soil with a generous amount of peat moss or vermiculite to keep the soil loose, and fill the pot three-quarters full with the soil mixture.
3. Place the bulbs on the surface of the soil without pressing them in. (Pressure could cause root damage.) Pack additional soil around the bulbs, leaving the tops exposed.
4. Water thoroughly from the top or place the container in a small pan of water so that the soil slowly absorbs the water.
5. Store the plants for about twelve weeks in either a cool corner of the house without sunlight or in the basement. The best storage temperature is 45 to 60°F. Proper storage is important for good root development.
6. Check the plants periodically to make sure that they are kept damp, but do not soak the bulbs. When the bulbs show 1½- to 2-inch sprouts, place them in full sunlight. A window where the temperature range is 60 to 75°F is ideal. Within two to three weeks you will have beautiful blossoms.

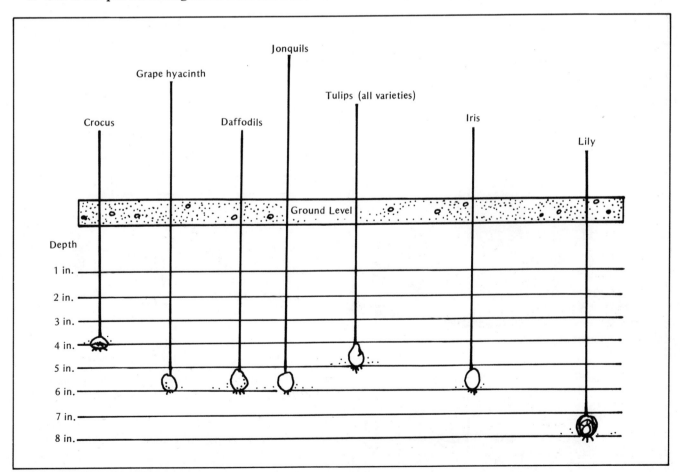

Appropriate depth to plant bulbs.

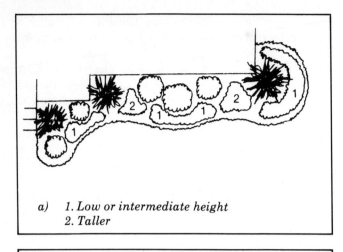

a)   1. Low or intermediate height
     2. Taller

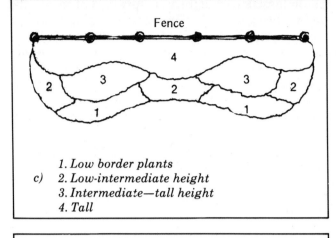

c)   1. Low border plants
     2. Low-intermediate height
     3. Intermediate—tall height
     4. Tall

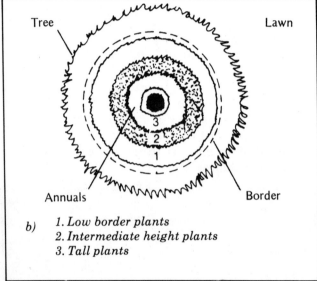

b)   1. Low border plants
     2. Intermediate height plants
     3. Tall plants

Annual planting designs a) foundation accents, b) around the base of a tree, c) garden area, and d) lawn accents

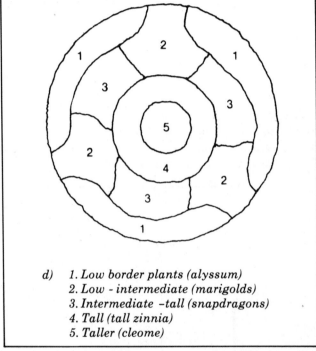

d)   1. Low border plants (alyssum)
     2. Low - intermediate (marigolds)
     3. Intermediate –tall (snapdragons)
     4. Tall (tall zinnia)
     5. Taller (cleome)

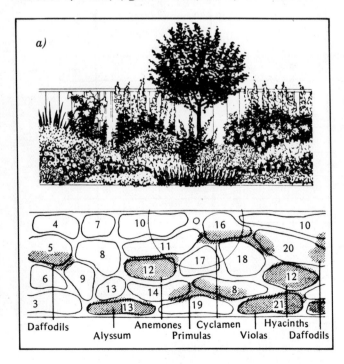

a)

Daffodils   Alyssum   Anemones   Primulas   Cyclamen   Violas   Hyacinths   Daffodils

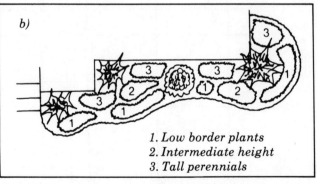

b)   1. Low border plants
     2. Intermediate height
     3. Tall perennials

Perennial plantings a) border planting, b) foundation planting

Vegetable Gardens

Growing your own vegetables not only is enjoyable but reduces your grocery bill. The quality and taste of home-grown vegetables cannot be equaled. For either a large or small garden, you must first develop a design and a planting schedule. Most residential areas provide enough space to grow at least enough tomatoes, lettuce, and carrots to supply a family for an entire season.

When planting, especially small gardens, you should choose crops that will produce the greatest yield in terms of pounds per square foot, such as beans, beets, broccoli, carrots, cabbage, corn, lettuce, onions, peppers, and peas. It is also important to choose plants that grow well together, that have roots that do not compete, and that are mutually beneficial.

Choose for your garden an area that offers full sun and good soil, even though you will add nutrients to it. Also be sure it is accessible to a water source. The diagrams on the following pages illustrate a variety of garden designs based on vegetables that produce a high yield.

Soil Preparation

Thorough soil preparation is very important to give plants the right growing conditions. In early spring when the soil is workable, turn the soil to a depth of 10 inches with a pitchfork or rototiller and remove large sticks, stones, or clumps of sod. Additional materials can improve the soil.

Organic Materials Use a shovel to cover the area with 1 to 3 inches of organic materials (peat moss, animal manure, ground bark, leaves, and grass clippings) and work them in to a depth of 2 to 4 inches. This material will open up heavy clay soils as well as bind light sandy soils. As it decomposes, it will improve drainage and air movement, which in turn will aid in the regulation of soil temperatures and retention of nutrients in the root zone.

Lime and Fertilizers Ground limestone (to sweeten the soil) and fertilizer (to provide nutrients) can be applied at the same time and should be worked into the top 4 to 6 inches of the soil. To accurately determine the amount of lime and elements your soil requires, take a sample to your nursery or to an agricultural school for testing.

Most vegetables do best in a neutral or slightly

ORGANIC MATERIALS FOR BEDS AND GARDENS

Material	Source	Use
manure	dairies, agricultural schools, nurseries	flower beds, gardens
peat	nurseries, bogs	flower beds, foundation plantings
mulch, wood chips	nurseries, public work crews	flowers, shrubs, fruits
leaves	your yard, public work crews	all acid-loving trees and shrubs
sawdust	saw mills, nurseries	strawberries, blueberries

acid soil. Soil condition is generally rated in terms of pH: 7 indicates a neutral soil; numbers below 7 indicate degrees of acidity; numbers above 7 indicate degrees of alkalinity. Your pH should run between 6 and 7. As a rule of thumb, apply ground limestone at a rate of 5 pounds per 100 square feet.

All complete or commercial fertilizers are labeled with the percentage of each primary nutrient—nitrogen, phosphorus, and potassium; but the most common and efficient are 5-10-5 and 5-10-10. Apply 5 pounds of fertilizer per 100 square feet.

POUNDS OF GROUND LIMESTONE NEEDED PER 1,000 SQUARE FEET TO RAISE pH

Existing pH	Sand to 6.5	to 7.0	Clay to 6.5	to 7.0
4.5	78	90	196	219
5.0	69	79	173	196
5.5	46	69	115	173
6.0	23	46	58	115
6.5	—	23	—	58

Superphosphate is an excellent source of phosphate, which is essential for flower and fruit production. This nutrient can be spread once a year, when fertilizing, at a rate of 5 pounds per 100 square feet.

Buying Seeds

Better department stores, garden centers, mail order houses, and agricultural supply stores carry packets of garden seeds. Most packets contain enough seeds for an area of up to 1,250 square feet.

For larger gardens, it is more economical to purchase seeds by the ounce. For example, one ounce of a finer seed, like onions, will have over a few thousand seeds, sufficient to plant the largest design shown with enough left over for several more plantings. It should be noted that all vegetable seeds should be stored in dry, airtight containers.

Planting

All vegetable plants are divided into two categories: hardy and tender. Seeds for hardy plants can be put into the ground in the early spring or early fall because they remain dormant during the winter and withstand slight frosts. Tender vegetables must be planted later in the spring because they cannot withstand even the slightest frost without showing some signs of damage. The following is a partial list of hardy and tender vegetables.

Actually, planting is the hardest part of growing a vegetable garden. Maintenance entails only one and one-half hours per week for a 15 x 10-foot plot, up to three hours per week for a 25 x 50-foot plot. Just follow these steps:
- Gently sprinkle once a day to allow the water to seep into the soil.
- As a side-dressing, fertilize every three to four weeks with 5-10-5.
- As weeds appear, either pull them by hand or with a cultivator.
- Apply a combination of insecticide and fungicide on a regular schedule (see package directions) to eliminate any problems.
- After harvesting, remove all annual plants and add them to your compost pile for use next season. Rototill or turn the soil with a pitchfork, add some organic materials, and let them settle until your next planting.

PLANTING AND HARVESTING DETAILS FOR VEGETABLES

	Seeds (or plants) for 100 ft. row	Distance in row—set or thin	Distance between rows for hand cultivation	Depth to plant seeds	When to Plant Range of days before or after average last freeze for one-time planting	Frost Resistance	When to Harvest
Asparagus	1 pkt. or 66 rooted crowns	18″	36″ between double rows	½″	30 days before	Hardy	Third year after seeding or first year after setting crowns, when spears are 6 to 10 inches long and head is tight. Harvest only 6 to 8 weeks in spring.
Bean, Lima (Pole)	½ lb.	36″	30″	1″	15 to 30 days after	Tender	When the seeds are green and tender, just before pods reach full size and plumpness.
(Bush)	1 lb.	3″	24″	1″			
Bean, snap (Pole)	½ lb.	36″	30″	1″	10 to 30 days after	Tender	Before pods are full size and while seeds are about one-quarter developed.
(Bush)	1 lb.	3″	24″	1″			
Beets	2 oz.	3″	18″	½″	30 days before to 30 after	½ hardy	When 1¼ to 2 inches in diameter.
Broccoli	1 pkt.	24″	30″	¼″	Up to 30 days before	Hardy	Before dark green blossom clusters begin to open.
Brussels Sprouts	⅛ oz.	18″	3′	¼″	30 days before to 60 after (for fall crop)	Hardy	Pick lowest sprouts on stem first. Keep leaves between sprouts picked off.
Cabbage	1 pkt. or 66 plants	18″	24″	¼″	45 to 20 days before	Hardy	When heads are solid and before they split.
Carrots	½ oz.	3″	18″	¼″	20 days before to 30 after	½ hardy	When root is 1 to 1½ inches in diameter.
Cauliflower	1 pkt.	18″	24″	¼″	Up to 30 days before	½ hardy	Before heads are ricey or blemished. Tie outer leaves above head when curds are 2 to 3 inches in diameter.
Chard	2 oz.	6″	24″	½″	30 days before to 30 after	Hardy	When leaves reach desired size. Harvest and leave plants for further production all summer and fall.
Collard	1 pkt.	18″	30″	¼″	40 days before to 40 after	Hardy	Begin harvest when leaves are large but still tender; continue until winter. Fall frost sweetens flavor.
Corn, Sweet	1 pkt. (2 oz.)	10″	36″	½″	Up to 45 days after	Tender	When kernels are fully filled out and in milk stage; silks, dry and brown; tips of ears filled tight.
Cucumber	1 pkt.	48″ between hills	48″	½″	10 days after	Tender	Harvest daily when fruits are slender and dark green before color becomes light.
Eggplant	1 pkt.	24″	36″	½″	10 days after	Tender	When fruits are half grown, before color becomes dull.
Endive	½ oz.	6″	18″	¼″	Up to 30 days before	Hardy	When leaves reach desired size, before they toughen.
Kale	1 pkt.	12″	18″	¼″	Up to 40 days before; to mid-July for fall crop	Hardy	When leaves are young and tender.

Kohlrabi	½ oz.	4″	24″	¼″	30 days before to 10 after	Hardy	When crowns are 2 to 3 inches in diameter.
Lettuce							
(Leaf)	½ oz.	3″	18″	¼″	30 days before to 30 after	½ hardy	When leaves reach desired size, are still tender.
(Head)	1 pkt.	8 to 12″	18″	¼″	Up to 30 days before	½ hardy	When heads are round and firm.
Muskmelon	1 pkt. or 3 to hill	60″ between hills	48″	½″	Up to 30 days after	Very tender	When stem easily slips from the fruit, leaving a clean scar.
Mustard Greens	½ oz.	3″	18″	¼″	30 days before to 10 after	Hardy	Use when leaves are large enough, but still tender.
Okra	2 oz.	12″	30″	½″	10 days before to 30 after	Tender	Pick pods while young before seeds harden.
Onion Sets	2 lbs.				Up to 45 days before	Hardy	For fresh table use, when ¼ to 1 inch in diameter; for boiling, when bulbs are 1½ inch; for storage, when tops fall over, shrivel at neck of bulb.
Dry (seed)	½ oz.	3″	18″	¼″			
Green (plants)	4 bunches						
Parsley	½ oz.	4″	24″	¼″	Up to 30 days before	Hardy	Any time after leaves reach desired size. Leave in garden for winter harvest.
Parsnip	1 oz.	3″	24″	¼″	Up to 20 days after	Hardy	After sharp frost. Roots may be safely left in ground over winter and used following spring.
Peas	1 lb.	2″	24″	1″	Up to 40 days before	Hardy	When pods are firm and well-filled but before seeds reach fullest size.
Peppers	1 pkt. or 66 plants	18″	30″	¼″	15 days after	Tender	When fruits are solid and have reached almost full size.
Potatoes	10 lbs.	12″	30″	4″	40 days before to 10 after	½ hardy	When tubers are large enough. Tubers continue to grow until vines die.
Pumpkin	1 oz.	60″ between hills	48″	½″	15 days after	Tender	When well-matured on vine. Skin should be hard and not easily punctured. Cut with portion of stem.
Radish	1 oz.	1″	18″	¼″	40 days before to 20 after	Hardy	Pull when they become of usable size.
Rhubarb	40 plants	30″	48″	1″	15 days after (seeds); 40 days before (crowns)	Hardy	Do not harvest the first year and for only a few weeks the second year. Then 8 to 10 weeks in spring.
Spinach	2 oz.	4″	18″	¼″	Up to 40 days before	Hardy	Use as soon as leaves are large enough.
Squash							
Summer (Bush)	1 oz.	60″ between hills	48″	½″	Up to 30 days after	Tender	In early immature stage when skin is soft, before seeds ripen.
Winter (Vine)	1 oz.	72″ between hills	48″	½″	Up to 30 days after	Tender	When well-matured on vine and skin is hard. Cut fruit off with portion of stem before frost.
Sweet Potatoes	50 plants	24″	30″		20 days after	Tender	Dig before first frost in the fall or just after frost.
Tomato	40 to 66 plants or 1 pkt.	36″ (unstaked) 18″ (staked)	48″ 48″	½″	Sow seeds 6 weeks before indoors. Set plants 10 days after.	Tender	When fruits are uniform red, but before they become soft.
Turnip	½ oz.	6″	18″	¼″	30 days before. Up to 6 weeks before first expected frost for fall crop.	Hardy	When 2 to 3 inches in diameter.

Chart courtesy of Thompson's Nursery and Garden Center

Herbs

If you want a little spice in your life, try growing some herbs. Herbs are grouped into annuals (basil, anise), biennials (parsley), and perennials (most of the popular herbs). Perennials are planted from late spring to early fall and will produce well-developed plants the following year. Annuals and biennials are usually planted in May. The twelve most popular herbs throughout the country are anise, basil, chives, dill, oregano, parsley, marjoram, sage, thyme, savory, mint, and rosemary. The outstanding feature of these popular plants is that their numbers can be increased by simple root cuttings done by removing the plant from the ground and dividing it into two or more equal parts.

Herbs love a soil that is slightly acid, well drained and moderately sandy. Fertility can be maintained by adding approximately 1½ pounds of a 10-6-4 fertilizer in ½-pound applications every six weeks starting in April. (This estimate is based on a 50-square-foot lot, sufficient for a family of two.)

For the average family of four, only three or four plants of each desired herb will provide more than enough for home use (based on a 100-square-foot lot). Fresh clippings can be taken every two to three weeks from early summer to late fall. Otherwise, new growth should be pinched back (taken off) when it reaches a length of 4 or 5 inches.

Drying Herbs You can enjoy your home-grown herbs during the winter months by drying them in one of two ways.

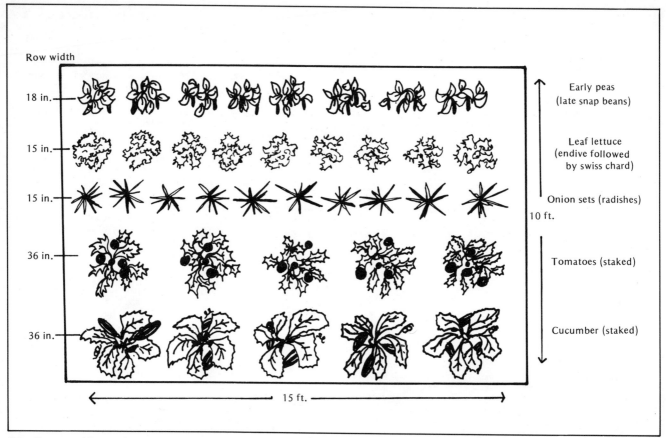

Row width

18 in. — Early peas (late snap beans)

15 in. — Leaf lettuce (endive followed by swiss chard)

15 in. — Onion sets (radishes)

36 in. — Tomatoes (staked)

36 in. — Cucumber (staked)

10 ft.

← 15 ft. →

Small vegetable garden design.

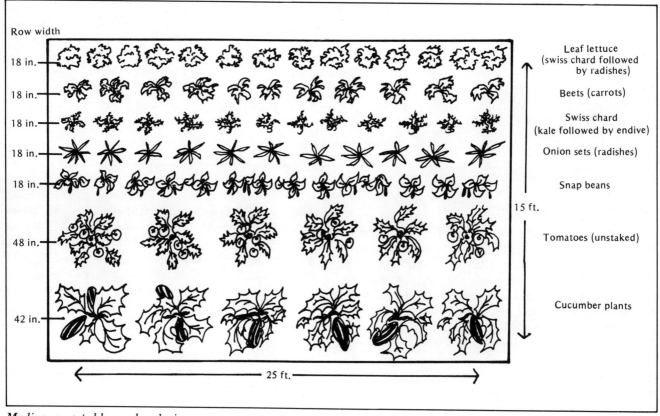

Row width

18 in. — Leaf lettuce (swiss chard followed by radishes)

18 in. — Beets (carrots)

18 in. — Swiss chard (kale followed by endive)

18 in. — Onion sets (radishes)

18 in. — Snap beans

48 in. — Tomatoes (unstaked)

42 in. — Cucumber plants

15 ft.

← 25 ft. →

Medium vegetable garden design.

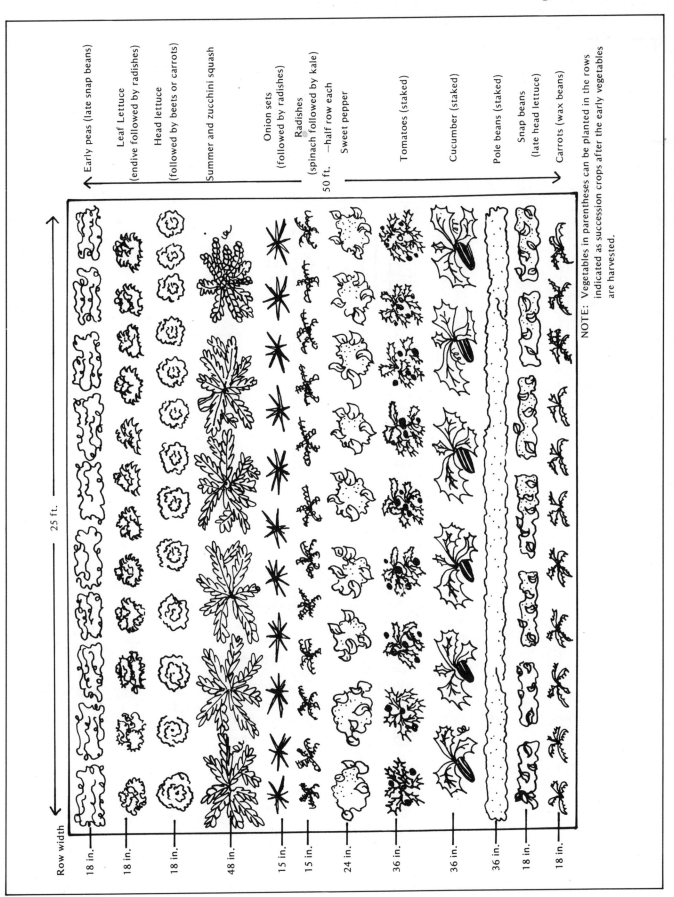

Early peas (late snap beans)

Leaf Lettuce
(endive followed by radishes)

Head lettuce
(followed by beets or carrots)

Summer and zucchini squash

Onion sets
(followed by radishes)

Radishes
(spinach followed by kale)
—half row each

50 ft.

Sweet pepper

Tomatoes (staked)

Cucumber (staked)

Pole beans (staked)

Snap beans
(late head lettuce)

Carrots (wax beans)

NOTE: Vegetables in parentheses can be planted in the rows indicated as succession crops after the early vegetables are harvested.

25 ft.

Row width

18 in.

18 in.

18 in.

48 in.

15 in.

15 in.

24 in.

36 in.

36 in.

36 in.

18 in.

18 in.

Large vegetable garden design.

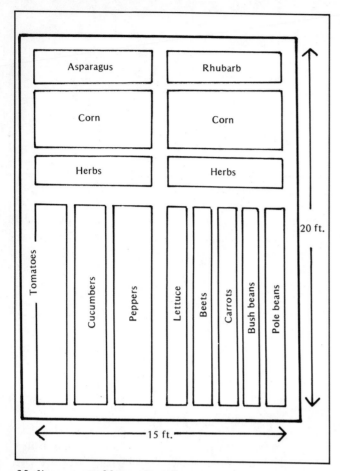

Medium vegetable garden plan.

Row width	
4 ft.	Rhubarb/onion
6 ft.	Raspberry
4 ft.	Strawberry
4 ft.	Asparagus
4 ft.	Carrots/lettuce (head)
4 ft.	Early peas/beets
4 ft.	Cabbage
2 ft.	Lettuce (leaf)/radish
3 ft.	Corn (early)
2 ft.	Pole beans
3 ft.	Corn late
½ ft.	Potato
½ ft.	Spinach
1 ft.	Onions
3 ft.	Tomato
3 ft.	Tomato

25 ft.   50 ft.

Large vegetable garden plan.

- Air Drying—This natural drying method is done by placing the thoroughly washed herbs in a piece of cheesecloth or similar material and hanging them outside to dry. When you are sure all the moisture has been drawn out of them, store the herbs on a rack made of window screening in a warm, dry area of the house devoid of sunlight, such as the attic or basement. Herbs that have larger stems can be strung and hung up to dry. Make sure that there is plenty of ventilation to aid in the drying process, and at the end of four to eight weeks the herbs should be ready for storage.
- Oven Drying—Instead of curing the herbs over a period of time, you can place them on the window screening and heat at 100 to 125°F until completely dried out. (Leave the oven door ajar.) Pulverize the dried herbs by hand-rubbing, discarding all stems, and place the herbs in a jar for storage. If any condensation forms on the inside of the jar, usually within twenty-four to thirty-six hours, dry the herbs longer.

Decks, Patios, Fences, and Accessory Structures

With the recent trend toward more leisure time, decks and patios have become an integral part of the outdoor living area. You can build a concrete patio or wooden deck that is functional yet attractive, and even a little unusual, by selecting an irregularly shaped structure and incorporating planting areas into your basic design. At the same time, try to keep it as natural as possible to blend in with your landscape. If your structure is of architectural interest, it will add beauty to your yard while providing additional living space for entertaining or relaxing.

Decks

No matter where you live, the addition of a deck will blend your indoor and outdoor living areas into one entity. By adding a deck to the main level of your home, you can inexpensively transform unlevel or inaccessible land into an extension of your indoor living areas. The beauty of a deck is that it is an affordable, low-maintenance structure that is sure to add elegance to your yard as well as value to your property.

Lumber Redwood is preferred for deck construction because of its durability and resistance to insects and decay. Cedar is also an excellent wood for decks, but it must be treated. Pine can be used, but it is generally not recommended because it is too soft and can decompose rather quickly.

- Grade A, Select—construction lumber is the strongest and most durable stock for decks, although this quality material may contain slight mill blemishes or tightly compacted knots.
- Grade B, Common—construction lumber contains more noticeable imperfections such as larger knots and mill blemishes. The greatest advantage of this wood grade is that it often contains a more highly textured grain, which in some instances makes it more desirable for garden uses.
- Merchantable (economy) Grade—lumber contains large, loose knots and many imperfections. It is not recommended for deck use but may be recut for the construction of a small wall or walk.

Finishes A good water repellent is recommended by all deck manufacturers. It should be applied before the deck is assembled to ensure full coverage of the wood. Creosote is an excellent wood preservative that deeply penetrates the stock to protect it from rot and most insects. Avoid skin contact; creosote will burn skin. Wood bleach will act as a catalyst to speed up the natural gray appearance achieved through weathering.

Stains can be used to suit your own taste and will not disturb the wood's texture or grain. However, never use a varnish or any other finish that forms a coat on the wood unless it is specifically recommended for deck use. These finishes will deteriorate when exposed to the elements and destroy the deck's appearance.

Deck Structure

- Footings—Precast concrete footings set into the ground or poured cement footings in holes below the frost line (3 to 4 feet) support the completed structure.
- Posts and Post Fillings—Posts are vertical wooden supports that are anchored to the footings. Many types of post anchors are available at building supply stores. Two common methods used to secure the posts are illustrated. The post can be (a) toenailed to a redwood block set in concrete or (b) secured with a drift pin to conceal the post anchorage.
- Beams—Beams of non-stress-graded lumber are secured to the posts with nails or metal connectors. Most ordinances require that a deck be designed to support 40 pounds per square foot plus the weight of the deck materials.
- Joists—The joists, which bear less weight than the beams, can be seated on the beams or attached flush with their tops. If seated on the beams, the joists may be toenailed. If set flush, angle irons or joist hangers should be used.
- Ledgers—To join one side of the deck to the house, a ledger is used to support the joists. While a 2-inch thick ledger may suffice, thicker ledgers will provide better bearing and easier toenailing. To prevent water from entering your home, position the ledge so that the deck surface will be at least one inch below the interior floor level.
- Decking—It is recommended that 2 x 4s or 2 x

6s be used for the decking floor (see table). Several arrangements of joists and decking planks to achieve different deck shapes and patterns are illustrated.

SUGGESTED BEAM SPANS

Beam Size	Grade	Width of Deck			
		6'	8'	10'	12'
		Span	Span	Span	Span
4 x 6	Select	6'6"	6'0"	5'0"	4'0"
	Common	4'6"	4'0"	3'6"	3'0"
4 x 8	Select	9'0"	8'0"	7'0"	6'0"
	Common	6'0"	5'0"	4'6"	4'0"
4 x 10	Select	11'6"	10'0"	8'6"	7'6"
	Common	7'6"	6'6"	6'0"	5'6"

SUGGESTED JOIST SPANS

Joist Size		Select or Common
2 x 6	16" o.c.	6'0"
	24" o.c.	5'0"
	36" o.c.	4'0"
2 x 8	16" o.c.	9'0"
	24" o.c.	7'6"
	36" o.c.	6'0"
2 x 10	16" o.c.	13'0"
	24" o.c.	11'0"
	36" o.c.	9'0"

(o.c. means "on center")
Deflection limited to L/240

SUGGESTED DECKING SPANS

Size	Grade	Span
2 x 4	Select or Common	24"
2 x 6	Select or Common	36"

Building a Deck You can build a 10 x 12-foot attached deck by following these six steps. In addition to the lumber, you will need a handsaw, drill, carpenter's square, level, an assortment of 16-penny nails and ⅜ x 6-inch lag screws, ten metal joist hangers, and five precast concrete footings or cement for pouring five footings.

1. Attach with lag screws a 12-foot skirt board

After: Built from the economical garden grades of California redwood, the deck extends well into the wooded yard behind this suburban home, creating 640 square feet of versatile living space out of a previously little-used sloping backyard. Photo courtesy of California Redwood Association

Before: The only connection between the house and the yard was a narrow stairway from the kitchen. Predominant in the sloping yard was a drainage trench which has been hidden by the deck construction. Turning a sloping site into versatile living space is one of the most dramatic applications of redwood decks. Photos courtesy of California Redwood Association

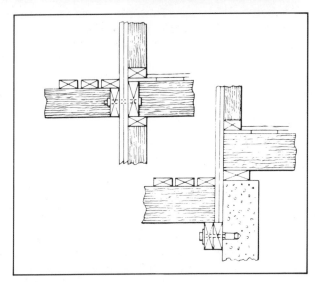

Ledgers a) normal 2-inch ledger, b) thicker ledger positioned below floor level.

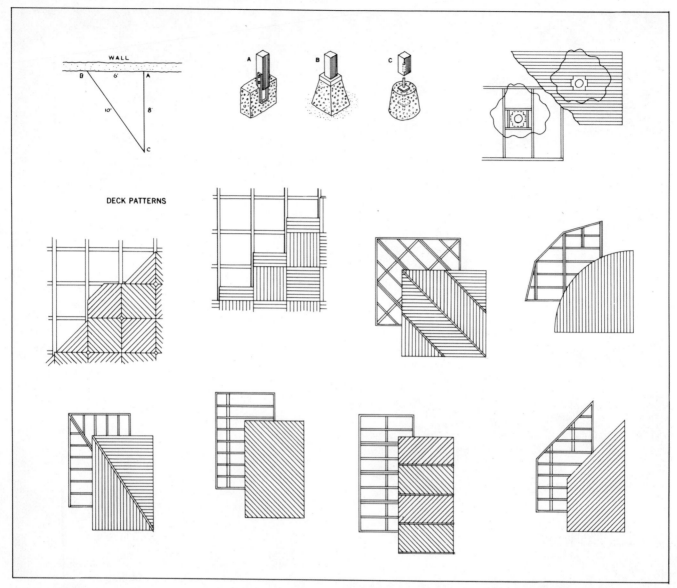

DECK PATTERNS

(beam) to the house stud or foundation, taking care that the final deck level will be at least 1 inch below the level of the interior floor. Establish a right angle from the house and measure out 10 feet 3¼ inches. Mark this spot with a stake (the position of one corner of the deck). Next, measure to the other corner and mark with a stake. Now make sure the whole area is square.

2. Dig five holes, 3- to 4-feet deep, positioned as illustrated, to receive the concrete footings. Set in precast footings or pour the cement directly into the holes. Whether or not posts are to be used and their length will depend upon the grade of your yard. If the posts are omitted, measure from the bottom of the skirt board to determine how deep the footings must be placed. If posts are required, attach to the footings, then place a board from the anchored skirt board to the top of the posts and use a level to

Above are popular deck patterns. The small illustration in the upper left corner shows a method for achieving square corners. (A, B, and C) are various examples of foundation footings.

ensure the proper height. Cut the posts 1⅝ inches below the correct height.

3. Attach the remaining skirt board to the posts with lag screws.

4. After checking position with a level, nail the skirt boards in place with 16-penny nails. It is advisable to predrill all nail holes that are close to the edge to prevent splitting of the wood.

5. Attach five 2 x 6 joists, 2 feet on center, 1⅝ inches below the skirt boards using metal joist hangers. Next, bolt the 2 x 4s along each of the 10-foot skirt boards, 1⅝ inches below the top.

6. Now you are ready to lay the deck. Use 2 x 4s (approximately 32) to cover the surface (about 400 lineal feet), spaced the width of a 16-penny nail.

a.

c.

d.

b.

Square, rectangular, and round precast concrete patio slabs can be bought at building supply centers, garden centers, and concrete products plants. At the left are shown the steps for installing square slabs. a) The patio area is staked off and a line is strung between the stakes. (Take into consideration the dimensions of the slabs so that none will have to be cut.) Remove sod and soil to a depth equal to that of the slab plus 2 or 3 inches for a sand subbase. b) Spread a layer of sand 2 or 3 inches deep and tamp it down thoroughly. Set screed boards in the sand to ensure a level, smooth base. (The finished patio should slope very slightly away from the house foundation so that water will run off.) c) Level the sand by running a straight board over the screed boards and removing excess sand. Screed boards should then be removed. d) Starting at a corner, set the precast slabs on the sand subbase. Butt the joints together. As a final step, sweep sand into all the joints. Photo courtesy of Portland Cement Company

Exposed aggregate concrete and redwood strips were used to build this deluxe deck. Photo courtesy of Portland Cement Company

Patios

A patio, like a deck, is a welcome addition to any outdoor living area and can be made in virtually any size, shape, or color.

Patio Blocks and Slabs Precast patio blocks or slabs, in a variety of colors and shapes, can be purchased at any lumberyard or building supply center. The advantages of these blocks are that they are easier to install than poured concrete, and they can be installed all at once or over a period of time as your pocketbook allows. Although patio blocks can be laid on unprepared ground, it is advisable to lay them in sand to avoid shifting.

- Preparing the Area—Stake out the area and dig out all grass and debris to a depth of 4 to 6 inches. If the patio is to be extremely large or uniquely shaped, you may want to use a form to ensure the proper level. Lay in 2 to 3 inches of sand over the entire surface, wet the sand, and then tamp or walk it down. Use a straight-edged 2 x 4 or similar board to level the sand.

- Setting the Blocks—Lay the first block at a corner where you can determine the proper level, then lay one row at a time so you can make leveling adjustments where needed. It is advisable to space blocks ¼ inch apart to add strength to the patio area.

Heavily wet the patio and let set until completely dry. If the sand settles after a few days, it may be necessary to repack in between the blocks.

Poured Concrete A poured patio requires more work than the precast blocks to install; and unless you are experienced, it is recommended that you seek professional advice to avoid making a mistake that will become part of the permanent structure.

- Preparing the Area—Prepare the area as you would for the patio blocks. Make a form around the entire area using 2 x 4s, staking every 3 feet for reinforcement. If you plan to make any curves in your form, use strapping and stake at 1-foot intervals to offset the increased stress on the thinner wood. It is best to drive all stakes slightly below the top of the form so they won't interfere when a straightedge is used in the leveling step. After the form has been completed, check to make sure it is level. (Allow an ⅛-inch slope for drainage.)
- Pouring the Concrete—You can purchase ready-mix concrete (just add water); mix sand and concrete yourself (3 parts sand to 1 part concrete); or have your concrete poured by a producer (who will add colored dye if desired).

Fill the form completely and level with a straightedge. If you have a bull-float, use it to further level any ridges left by the straightedge.

When all the surface water has evaporated, round all edges with an edging tool to safeguard against chipping. Next, using a jointer, make expansion lines about every 4 feet. Expansion lines reduce the stress on the concrete, which will in turn reduce the chances of cracking.

Colored square and rectangular patio blocks create an attractive, easily installed patio. Photo courtesy of National Concrete Masonry Association

Poured concrete was used to form this semicircular patio. Photo courtesy of Portland Cement Company

The final step is floating. The floating tool is used to establish an even, durable, skid-resistant surface.

- Curing—As soon as it is possible without damaging the surface, begin curing. Curing is the key to durability; lack of moist curing can cut the potential strength of concrete by as much as one half. Here are two simple methods: (1) keep surface moist by spraying or by covering with moistened burlap; (2) prevent moisture loss by laying curing paper, or polyethylene film, or by spraying a membrane curing compound. Curing with water is the most effective means, and is simplest. If sprinkling is chosen, use a fine spray applied continuously. At temperatures of 50 to 70°F, curing should continue for at least seven days; for 70°F or higher, cure for at least five days.

Fences

When choosing a fence, first decide what function it will serve. Will it be used for privacy, visual appeal, or to admit or control sunlight or air? Whatever its purpose, a fence, if properly selected, can add charm and enduring beauty to your yard.

Most fences are made of redwood, cedar, or pine and can be purchased in preassembled sections. All that is required is setting the posts and inserting the panels.

If you plan to dig the holes yourself, it is wise to rent a post-hole digger from a local rental shop. Some fence companies will supply this tool for a limited time when a fence is purchased.

The following is a step-by-step plan for installing three of the basic preassembled fences—stockade, post and rail, and hurdle:

1. Drive stakes in the ground at each end of the line to be fenced. Stretch a strong string tightly between them a few inches above the ground, and 1 or 2 inches on your side of the property line. This is your guide for setting the posts in a straight line.
2. Dig your first posthole at one end of the fence line. The holes should be at least 9 inches in diameter. For a 3-foot-high fence, the holes should be about 28 inches deep; for a 4-foot-high fence, 30 inches; and for a 6½-foot fence, about 34 inches deep.
3. Place an end pole (holes on one side) in the posthole and set it so that it touches the line you have stretched. Fill in the hole, at the same time tamping it firmly so that the post stands in a plumb position.
4. Insert one of the fence sections into the hole to locate the next posthole. Remove the section and dig the hole.
5. After you have dug the hole, insert the fence section. When the section has been secured in place, nail the ends of the rails into the first pole using 10-penny galvanized nails.
6. Insert the next pole, backfill the hole, and nail the section to the pole.
7. Repeat the above steps until the fence is completed.

Post and Rail When the ground is uneven, don't set the fence so that it looks choppy. Try to get a smooth (not necessarily level but smooth) line on the post tops by setting some posts deeper, or less deep than standard. Cut or fill under fence.

On sloping ground be sure to erect the posts in a plumb position. The rails should then follow the slope of the ground. You will find that the holes in the posts are a little larger than the turned ends of the rails. This allows the rails to be raised, lowered, or swung from side to side several inches. In extreme cases the pin can be shaved off to allow for a very steep slope.

Hurdle On gently sloping ground this type of fence looks well even if the sections lean downhill a bit.

On a steep slope the fence will look better if the posts and center brace are kept vertical (plumb) and the rails are parallel to the surface of the ground. To accomplish this it is necessary to remove the diagonal braces so the fence sections can be "racked" to fit the grade. After the fence is erected, the braces can be nailed on again.

Stockade When the ground is uneven, again, don't set the fence so that it looks choppy.

Try to maintain a smooth, not necessarily level, line on the post tops by setting some posts deeper or less deep than standard. Cut or fill under fence.

Unless otherwise requested, you will find all your fence sections are built level. If your ground is sloping, you should "rack" the sections to fit your slope as follows:

This wood fence provides privacy and a windscreen for this pool and deck area.

Close-up of two rails in a post. The posthole is larger than the rails to allow rails to be raised or lowered to fit a slope.

Completed post and rail fence.

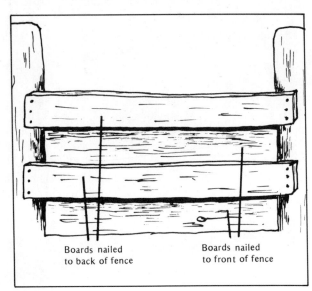

Horizontal board divider with boards on front and back of posts.

Typical gate latch hardware.

1. Work downhill if possible.
2. Fasten section into plumb post.
3. Exert downward pressure on end of section before attaching post.
4. When finished, all posts and pickets should be plumb. Rails should follow the slope of the ground.

Horizontal Board Divider If you prefer to build your own fence, a horizontal board divider is an excellent addition to any landscape.

1. Space posts (4 x 4s) 4 feet apart and anchor them in cement at a depth of 32 inches.
2. With 16-penny galvanized nails, nail a 1 x 8-inch board across the posts at ground level.
3. From the top of the board, measure up 8 inches and mark with a pencil. This is where the bottom of the next board will rest.
4. Nail the second board across the posts in the same manner as the first. Continue these steps until you have reached the desired height.
5. From the back of the fence, nail in all other 1 x 8-inch boards in an alternating pattern to fill in open spaces left by front boards.

The completed fence not only will give you privacy but will allow air to flow through it.

Gates Gates receive the most abuse so make sure that you use good quality hardware that will take punishment. All latches and hinges should be corrosion resistant and heavy duty. Allow a 3-inch clearance between the fence and gate so it will swing freely. All hardware is reversible, so the gate can be installed to open either in or out and from either the left or right.

Outdoor Lighting

An outdoor lighting system serves two important purposes: it extends the pleasure you derive from your landscape design into the evening hours, and it provides a low-cost security system for your home.

Your choice of fixtures should match your own taste as well as the existing landscape. For example, in a formal setting, in-ground or flood-type fixtures are more pleasing than hanging lanterns strung around the yard. Select your lighting carefully so that it will enhance rather than detract from the beauty of your outdoor living areas.

Lights mounted on the roof or away from the house to illuminate flower gardens and foundation plantings will guard your doors and windows against unwelcome intruders. On larger lots you may find that you still have some shadowed areas that are best illuminated by a few wide-angle floodlights installed far enough away from the house to totally light up the area. A well-lit yard is a good deterrent against a burglar whose entry could go undetected in the dark.

It is wise to purchase outdoor fixtures at hardware or electrical stores that provide information on proper use and installation to meet product and electrical code requirements. For example, outdoor fixtures are designed and labeled for certain wattage, generally for up to 150-watt bulbs. You should carefully observe the specifications to avoid damage to the fixture or an electrical fire.

The three basic types of outdoor lighting fixtures—in-ground, hanging, or pole—can be fitted with a variety of colored bulbs to make your outdoor area even more attractive. With the exception of lanterns, better quality hanging fixtures are made of die-cast aluminum and are designed for rugged, prolonged use.

In-Ground Lighting Perhaps the least expensive but most effective way to accent walkways or garden areas is with the use of an in-ground fixture, which can be permanently or temporarily installed, is completely weatherproof, and will accommodate up to 150-watt bulbs. The most common of these fixtures is the spike-light, which is fitted with a spike on its base so that it will rest flat on the ground. The cord is 25 feet long and should be plugged into an outdoor receptacle or an extension made for heavy-duty outdoor use.

In-ground lights can be used to illuminate shrubs, entrances, Christmas trees, or lawn decorations.

Hanging Lights Traditionally known as floodlights or spotlights, these lamps were at one time used primarily to light up doorways or garages. With increased evening use of outdoor areas, however, hanging lights have become the chief source of illumination for all-around use. They are available in a variety of holders for single bulbs or multibulb arrangements.

Canopy-lights are units that have a mounting plate on them for easy attachment on patios, porches, or under the eaves. They come complete with leads, mounting straps, screws, and canopy. The sleeve of the lamp is long enough to protect the neck of the bulb from any damage.

Lamp holders are designed for heavy-duty use in any weather condition. A spring-loaded swivel mounting allows you to position the light in any direction. Lamp holders are easily mounted on any standard outlet box or canopy-type fixture and come complete with threaded stem, leads, and lock nut.

Shaded spotlights are similar to lamp holders, but the bulb is completely recessed in a sleeve that protects it under adverse conditions.

Lanterns are popular hanging fixtures for informal lighting. They are made of colored plastic sleeves strung together for convenient hanging. Regular light bulbs are used in these fixtures. However, 60 watts is the maximum wattage recommended, otherwise the plastic sleeves could melt or cause an electrical fire. Although not an effective source of light for all-around garden use, they are excellent for lighting patios or porches.

Pole lamps are used extensively to accent walks or patio areas. Most fixtures come completely fitted with glass, chimney, and wired electric socket. They can be made of either wood or metal. Wooden poles should have a preservative applied to them before installation.

The pole can be set in the ground by backfilling around the base, setting it in cement, or setting it on a reinforced cleat. Although many contractors recommend running the cable in a length of plastic pipe, a metal pipe will be better able to withstand the pressure of a concrete patio or walkway and will protect the wires from being punctured should you later dig in the cable area.

This most popular form of outdoor lighting can be purchased in many styles as well as colors. The average fixture will cost about $60, not including the electrical work; but a custom-made lamp could cost considerably more.

Index